Kelly P. Campbell, CFP®, CMFC®, ChFC®, AIF®

"Live the Life you Deserve"

700 South Washington Street, Suite 220
Alexandria, VA 22314
703-535-5300 Fax: 703-535-5317

kelly@campbellwealth.com   www.campbellwealth.com

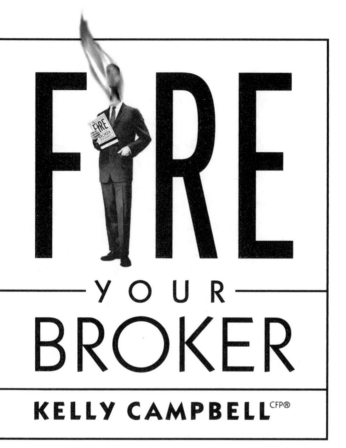

FIRE
— YOUR —
BROKER

KELLY CAMPBELL^{CFP®}

Fire Your Broker™
Copyright © 2009 by Kelly Campbell
www.fireyourbroker.com

ISBN-13: 978-0-9840994-0-5
ISBN-10: 0-9840994-0-9

Published by:
Riverfront Press, LLC
PO Box 3044, Merrifield, VA 22116
FIRST EDITION, JULY 2009

Cover and Interior Layout by:
AGW Idea Group, Inc.
www.AGWIdeaGroup.com

Printed in the United States of America

NOTE TO READERS

TABLE OF CONTENTS

DEDICATION

This book is dedicated to those financial advisors around the country who are truly and honestly committed to their clients, advisors who celebrate the victories with them and suffer along with them in times of challenge.

The book is also dedicated to my trophy wife, Kim. She is a trophy in every sense of the word except I didn't marry her just because she looked great on my arm. I married her because she was and is the most extraordinary woman I have ever known. She's been wonderfully understanding of her focused, ambitious husband who works too much, exercises too much, travels too much, and is too opinionated. I am most grateful to her and would not enjoy nearly the level of success that I have today without her.

Thank you Kim.

PREFACE

As chairman and CEO of the nation's leading independent broker/dealer, I know from experience the value of unbiased advice in helping investors reach important financial objectives. Each day I witness first-hand the positive impact made by financial advisors who take the time and care to incorporate their clients' life goals, cherished dreams, and personal passions into a solid financial plan. Now, more than ever, this degree of personal attention is essential to helping you to make sound financial decisions.

Most of us spend a great deal of time researching and reviewing our options when deciding which home or car to buy or where to go for vacation. The time and effort spent on these decisions should certainly be no greater than the thought you give to finding the right financial advisor, particularly when you consider that the stakes are significantly higher.

Today, understanding and responding to market conditions is more challenging than at any point in recent years. At the same time, the variety of available products has never been greater. Amidst so much uncertainty, it is critical to work with a financial advisor who looks out for your best interests and makes recommendations that support your financial goals and personal values. You need truly independent advice, delivered without conflict or personal agenda, to help you make some of the most impactful decisions of your life.

In the years since Kelly Campbell joined LPL Financial, I have been tremendously impressed by the growth of his practice, which has been propelled forward by his unwavering focus on the client and his ability to offer comprehensive advice. Kelly's commitment to his life's work truly sets him apart from so many others. And the enthusiasm Kelly brings to his practice is a trait every investor should demand of a financial advisor.

Fire Your Broker will help you to learn what to look for in the financial advisor with whom you entrust your money and your future. You will discover that a good advisor puts the interest of the client above all other considerations; that a good advisor cares about helping you to attain not simply your financial goals, but also your personal goals; and that a good advisor asks questions that actually help you to better understand yourself as you discover (or rediscover) the dreams that can make your life truly rewarding.

I hope that each person who reads this book takes Kelly's lessons to heart and puts his recommendations into practice. Making the effort to find the right advisor may well be the best financial decision you ever make.

Mark S. Casady
Chairman and Chief Executive Officer
LPL Financial

(Author's note: LPL Financial is the largest independent broker/dealer in the U.S.)

INTRODUCTION

You can thank Bernie Madoff for this book.

Although there are a great many superb financial advisors in this country, there are also a great many people posing as financial advisors who don't have the training, resources, insight, ethics and/or intellect to be in the business.

You give these individuals your money, your life savings, your retirement funds, and ask them to keep that money safe and make it grow, but all too often, that does not happen.

So how can the average investor tell if their advisor is capable or incompetent or even a crook?

In my almost twenty years as a financial advisor I have been witness to some catastrophic strategies employed by incompetent advisors. I've seen people victimized by brokers more interested in making money for themselves than for their clients. I've commiserated with people who trusted the wrong person and lost everything.

And I'm sick of it.

The recent case of Bernard Madoff illustrates two critical questions: 1) How can a respected financial advisor scam his clients out of a reported $50 billion and 2) How can an investor know the signs that his financial advisor may not be doing what he or she is supposed to be doing? After all, Madoff's clients were the rich and famous, people controlling huge amounts of money, people assumed to be among the most sophisticated investors in the world. And yet he conned them into monumental losses.

That despicable action pushed me to write this book.

Bernard Madoff, or Bernie as his former friends called him, changed the financial brokerage industry for everyone. By his actions he called into question the honesty and character of everyone in the industry. He infected the public with the perception that all financial advisors cannot be trusted. In my mind, he is to the financial industry what Mad Cow Disease is to the beef industry.

The doubt created by Madoff is neither right nor fair but it is real. The best financial advisors among us can wring our hands in protest OR we can be proactive and demonstrate to the investing public that there is a tangible difference between good and bad advisors. What I've sought to do in this book is give you some measuring sticks, some principles and guidelines that will help you determine whether your current advisor is performing at a high standard or whether you should perhaps shop around for someone who operates their business in a more trustworthy and more profitable (for you) fashion.

So how is someone outside the industry supposed to know what evaluation criteria to use? I will tell you.

I'll be giving you a list of things to look for in your advisor. Understand that mine is not the only approach to financial planning, but it's not just opinion. What I'm telling you is based on my experience, but it's also information that is quantifiable and in most cases accepted as common practice at the highest levels of this profession. It's critical information needed to evaluate a financial advisor.

I will also tell you about certain practices within the industry that are an embarrassment to every advisor who operates an ethical, above-board business. There are "dirty little secrets" that some brokers use to make money...not for you, for themselves. Some of these trading schemes are riding the edge of ethical responsibility while others are completely illegal. I want you to realize that anyone's portfolio is subject to potential trading irregularities and knowing what to look for is your best defense.

A Little Perspective

In my years as a financial advisor I've been blessed with tremendous success. I believe that a major reason for this financial success is that I have a personal bond with my clients. I realized early on that the more I became emotionally invested in my clients, the harder I'd work for them and the more personally fulfilling their success would be for me.

I often appear on CNBC, *FOX Business*, ABC *Nightline* and other financial networks not only because my firm has been successful but because I try to remain on the cutting edge of the industry. My hope is that I can bring you, the investor, closer to understanding this industry when it's at its best and most current.

Many people want to give advice. They believe they have a story to tell or experiences that qualify them to instruct you how to do something. Being a Certified Financial Planner, Chartered Mutual Fund Counselor, Chartered Financial Consultant, and having my Registered Investment Advisor License creates an impressive alphabet soup on my business card. But education alone hardly qualifies me to offer the advice in this book.

My confidence that I have something worthwhile to say comes from my experience in the investment trenches. In nearly two decades in the financial services industry, I've met with literally thousands of people and heard as many stories. Those stories have completely shaped my thinking. I've had clients tell me things about their investing experience that I wanted to emulate, and I've heard stories where I was shocked and vowed, "I will never treat a client that way."

The experience ranges from having one of my first clients with two small children die in his early thirties, to helping one of my older clients and his wife literally prepare for his death. I've worked with people who deeply loved their kids and grandkids and with others who had disowned their children. I've helped people sell a business and deal with huge windfall profits; and I've worked with those who lost their jobs after 20 years of service, leaving them with no way to cover family expenses.

I've heard dozens of stories about fortunes lost by careless or inattentive financial advisors and complaints from clients who had the same advisor for years and never personally met him. I've heard of advisors churning accounts for commissions without regard for the client's welfare. I've heard tales of businesses lost, retirements squandered, elderly people who thought they were financially secure only to find out later that their advisor had made risky investments and lost.

I could go on for volumes because every client is different with unique challenges and needs.

Yet through all of those experiences, both good and bad, I realized that my calling in life is not just about a rate of return, or which insurance policy is the best, or when might be the right time to sell a company. It's not about helping minimize taxes or compounding interest.

I go to work each day because I believe I'm here for something much greater. I have been called to give people perspective. I know this because I have to constantly remind myself that I need perspective. I know how difficult it is to maintain.

Gaining perspective may not sound like much but it's actually one of the most valuable gifts anyone can receive. Perspective allows us to step back and think before making the wrong decision. It's the second opinion that makes your ultimate choices the best they can be. It allows you to think about how you want to be remembered or asks the question about whether you're living life to the fullest versus simply living day to day.

I hope to help people not only to think outside the proverbial box, but to step outside that stupid box and then **act** outside that box. Life is about goals and dreams and family and love for each other. Too often money gets in the way. I pray that I bring perspective to my clients' lives and then help them to live the life they deserve. I feel blessed that I can make a living doing exactly that.

Perspective is what many people need to help them determine if their investments are currently with the right person and firm. Choosing a great financial advisor is not easy, but it could be the most important step you take in your quest for financial independence. And keep in mind, it should be the very **first** step.

A Little History

So what gives me the right to tell you what you should look for in a good financial planner? I'm not a Harvard grad finishing at the top of my class. I didn't develop Portfolio Theory.

I'm perhaps more correctly described as a graduate of the school of hard work. I'm kind of a blue-collar financial planner if there is such a thing.

In truth, I was a solid 'B' student who went to college not knowing what I wanted to be when I grew up. Early in my career I actually was a blue-collar worker, not the owner of a multi-million dollar wealth management firm.

My background is very unassuming, very normal. When I was in grade school, I began working with a neighbor who had an auto-body and fender business. Most weekends and every summer for years, I would help him fix dents and paint cars for $3 an hour. It was fun and I learned a lot. As a matter of fact, I learned so much that after my entrepreneurial neighbor moved, I took over his business and began painting cars in my back yard.

I had no problem finding customers, and in the far corner of my parents' yard I would sand and paint cars right out in the open air. It probably wasn't an environmentally friendly approach and definitely not something my neighbors appreciated. But as time went on, I became very good at painting and was able to work my way through college as a "garage monkey."

The reason I didn't have a more outstanding grade point average in college was largely because I couldn't find any profession that inspired me, that created a passion to excel. It wasn't until the end of my undergraduate studies that I discovered the financial services industry. I knew that was my calling.

After finishing school I immediately got a job in financial services, but quickly realized that working on commission didn't bring in enough money. So I decided to paint cars on the side.

I remember getting up at 4:00 AM each day and going over to the garage I was renting to paint a car. Three hours later I would go back home, shower, clean the paint from under my fingernails, put on a suit and tie and go to the office to meet people and talk about their money. At around 7:00 PM, I'd go back to the garage, change clothes, clean up the car and have it ready for the owner to pick up the next morning. And I did this 5 or 6 days a week.

People depended on me to fix their dents while others depended on me to fix their finances. It was tough, but hard work was all I knew.

As I slowly became more successful in financial services, I began to phase out of the car-painting business. Once I began to focus my energy entirely on planning, my business began to take off. I met with more people, worked with larger accounts and began studying to be a Certified Financial Planner. The more I learned, the more I realized how much there was to learn and I became almost fanatical about continuing education. The "alphabet soup" after my name isn't the result of trying to impress anyone so much as a reflection of my profound realization that the more I know, the more I'll be able to help people.

About this same period I began to concentrate on working with baby boomers and seniors. To me this was the turning point in my career because I felt I was I truly focusing on my life's purpose: securing people's financial future.

A Big Promise

The real driving force for this "life purpose," indeed my passion for investment planning is based on a promise I made to my stepfather, Richard "Dick" Alley.

My father died when I was a teenager and my mother remarried this truly great man. He and I grew very close and I came to think of him as my Dad. A number of years ago, a situation developed in his life that changed it forever.

Dick had been retired for many years and was living well off a nice pension and investment accounts. He had a good friend who was also his stockbroker. Because of this "trusted" relationship the broker had the ability to make changes in my stepfather's account without consulting him. Unfortunately after some very prosperous times, this "friend" developed a drug habit and siphoned significant assets out of several of his clients' accounts, including my stepfather's. Dick lost about 80% of his portfolio, not because of market corrections, but due to the infidelity of his broker.

My stepfather and I had many conversations about that tragedy. I remember one conversation in particular that has guided me in my business and in my relationship with my clients.

Dick said, "Kelly, you have a big responsibility. You are investing people's money at the end of most of their working years. This is money that they will rely on for the rest of their lives. They can't go back to work; they can't earn it back if they lose it. So always remember to do the right thing for them."

These words are the foundation of what I do and why I do it. They are my guide and my inspiration for writing this book. Hopefully they can become an inspiration for many others in this profession.

Thank you, Dick. I will protect my clients.

CHAPTER 1

Choosing the Best Financial Advisor

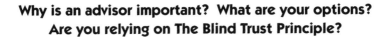

**Why is an advisor important? What are your options?
Are you relying on The Blind Trust Principle?**

Since the invention of an exchange system, responsible people have tried to be good stewards of their money. Over the last twenty years or more, individuals who've accumulated wealth have increasingly sought professional financial help to manage that wealth. Thus, the traditional equation has changed to: "Is your *financial advisor* a good steward of *your* money."

Unfortunately for the investing public, the answer too often is NO!

That's outrageous, because having your assets managed by someone who specializes in the field should be an unqualified positive. But because many brokers are either not qualified, don't have enough experience, can't offer all of the types of investment products that a client needs, or are more interested in making money for themselves than making money for you, the industry has suffered an identity crisis.

It doesn't need to be so.

To further complicate the financial picture, the turbulent stock market of late has many investors questioning the competence of their financial advisor. As a result of some frightening returns, investors are currently seeking or should be seeking a new advisor. And while this may seem a daunting task, it may be the best time. My goal is to simplify the process.

You'll quite likely hear advice like, "Don't change captains in a storm." But if the captain of your financial ship isn't demonstrating that he or she is in control in these dangerous waters it may be time to abandon ship. The time to find a new advisor may be right now.

New relationships often lead to new strategies, new investment plans, and significant portfolio changes. (Change can also signal serious tax consequences but while the market is lower, most of these tax considerations may be largely nonexistent.) Changing now may work in your favor on many levels.

Clearly there is huge dissatisfaction among investors. An article in *The Wall Street Journal*, October 4, 2008, quoted a survey by Price & Associates asserting that 81% of investors with over $1 million at risk planned to leave their current advisor. 86% planned to tell others to "avoid" their advisor. Fully 90% of "large brokerage" investors were planning to take their money from their advisor.

Even more startling, only 2% said they would recommend their current firm to a friend. There are far too many incompetents out there giving the profession a bad name. Clearly the atmosphere is ripe for a change.

Plus our pal Bernie changed the financial landscape forever.

The Madoff scandal taught us that we're not as safe as we once thought. How could one person fool so many people for so many years...and more importantly, how could he fool his overseeing regulatory agency, the Securities and Exchange Commission?

An investing environment that has been historically viewed as a "land of opportunity" now feels like it comes with a disclaimer: *caveat emptor*.

What's the investor to do?

There are some actions you can take to protect yourself; protect yourself until you can find someone who will protect your interests with the same diligence you would. This is not a survival of the fittest; it's a survival of the smartest. And being smart about how you choose an investment advisor could be crucial to your financial future.

Most People Need Help with Financial Management

Over the last 20 years, the United States S&P 500 Index has averaged a net return of 8.4% per year. In that same time frame the average individual investor was able to net an average return of 1.87%. Over 20 years the difference between an 8.4% and a 1.87% return is huge.

So why does the average individual not have more success? Simply put, they have a pack mentality and follow the market trends, buying when the market is high and selling when it's down. Most people simply aren't skilled with investing, they don't really know how to build a portfolio, they don't understand the range of options they have, and they tend to get very emotional about their investments.

Adding emotion to your investing almost guarantees poor decision making. Misplaced emotion prompts people to invest in things that have no real value; it makes people choose investments on a whim; and it makes them keep stocks far beyond when they should be sold.

In short, emotion motivates investors to buy high and sell low.

In one sense, investing is a zero-sum game. For every person who bought a stock at $10 and sold it for $100, there's someone else who bought the stock at $100 and sold it at $10. It's a competition of winners versus losers. Each investor is competing with all the other investors out there to determine what to buy and when. Unless you're a professional, you are sadly outgunned. As an untrained individual you are trying to pick stocks, bonds, various funds, etc. against people who do it for a living. Yes, it can sometimes be thrilling but it's seldom profitable.

If you needed heart surgery, would you do it yourself? Even if you were a seasoned heart surgeon, you'd seek out a skilled specialist and trust your life to that person. If you had the time, you'd be especially diligent in selecting your surgeon given the downside of a poor choice. You'd ask friends and other specialists, do research, and check the credentials of your potential doctor. You'd meet with the doctor and get a measure of his or her confidence and try to gauge experience and expertise. Why should it be different whether you're risking your life or your life's savings?

You should choose a financial planner/wealth manager with the same or more care that you'd choose your surgeon. After all, the threshold for even being called a surgeon is extremely high and the process is heavily monitored. Unfortunately the financial planning arena doesn't have the same kind of rigorous standards. Even so, selecting a great financial advisor doesn't have to be intimidating.

It's long been a passion of mine to educate people about the details of good financial planning. I frequently hold workshops for current and future clients to facilitate this goal. One question I always ask in my workshops: "Is the relationship you have with your advisor based on facts or is it based on blind faith?"

Too often people select their financial advisor because they play golf with them or heard from someone that so-and-so was good. Typically these would-be advisors have set up their businesses on the back of a cocktail napkin or they've evolved into planning from some related profession.

There are numerous people purporting to be financial planners who are actually trained as accountants or are just people with a business degree. They have no specific training in market analysis, no business plan, no marketing plan, and most importantly, no investment management plan. They just thought they could make money if they put up a "Financial Advisor" sign.

Don't Need an Advisor?

What are the alternatives for managing your nest egg?

We all know that your investments must grow. As a matter of fact, they really need to grow somewhat significantly because they have to outpace both inflation and taxes. If we assume a long-term inflation rate of 3.5% as well as a combination of federal and state taxes, you should typically have at least a 5.0% annual return to just keep pace with inflation after tax.

The point of investing, however, is not to break even; it's to create growth. That means we really need at least a 6–9% overall return.

Now remember, we are not talking about 6–9% each year, we're really talking about having an average over a number of years. In order to make a 6–9% return, you pretty much have to invest in equities for a portion of your portfolio and equities involve risk...risk in the form of fluctuation. This simply means your investments can be on something of a rollercoaster ride. Now, there are ways around that volatile ride but the odds of you figuring this out on your own are shaky at best. No offense.

With confidence being seriously low in the U.S. and abroad, you may decide to manage the money yourself anyway. Here are the most common ways individuals seek to preserve their wealth.

1) Under the mattress—For years people have talked about keeping their money under the mattress. This was a concept that evolved during the Great Depression in the era of failing banks and before the FDIC insured deposits. Hiding your money recently became more about having emergency cash on hand if you needed it. To keep it safe from bad guys you keep money under your mattress; the theory being that you would probably wake up if someone lifted your mattress. (Funny that I am writing this at 4:17 AM because I can't sleep; someone could be in my bedroom stealing my money even now because my wife is a sound sleeper.)

Even though it may be somewhat absurd to keep the bulk of your money under the mattress, it's not a bad idea to keep some cash in a safe place at home. Other ideas besides the mattress: an airtight bag in the tank of the toilet, in the pocket of a jacket in your closet (make sure your significant other doesn't take that jacket to the cleaners, you'll end up poorer but will get a Christmas card from your drycleaner), an envelope taped to the bottom of a shelf, or a random file in your filing cabinet. Try not to forget where you put it; the day you really need cash for the pizza guy you'll go hungry. But I digress...

2) Money in the bank—This is a good idea for some funds but not too much. As I mentioned earlier, your money needs to grow. Bank savings and checking accounts, CDs, Money Market Funds, or even so-called high-interest checking accounts really don't earn a very high rate. You'd be cutting into the bank's profit. After tax, you will **not** be outpacing inflation. And all I mean by that is your favorite bottle of Cabernet or dark beer will cost 3.5% more next year and you'll only have 2% more money. Simply putting your money in any bank-based fixed income account will mean that you'll not be able to purchase as much this year as you did last year. Money shrinks over time unless you're working to make it grow.

3) Buy a few individual stocks—Great, let's try to find the next Google, buy it at the bottom...only 85 bucks a share (8/04) and then hold it until the peak and sell it at the highest point to date: $747 a share (11/07). The problem is, what if you didn't sell (most people didn't)? The stock has come down as low as $247 in the past year. Wow, what a swing! Of course, profiting from that Google stock assumes you came up with that winner in the first place. Many stock investors choose several stocks and chance into a couple of winners along with a few losers. Unfortunately, they usually end up netting a very low or even negative return.

Note: if you're really committed to watching your investments but are not in the investment business, you'll usually be better off with a portfolio of mutual funds. As you'll see, the determining factors in choosing investments should first be grounded in choosing the allocation of types of investments. A secondary consideration is the choice of investment itself. That's right, I said it's not choosing the actual investment as the number one factor that determines your rate of return, it's the *mix* of types of assets that really counts.

4) You can hire a stockbroker—Many brokers will charge you a commission for the trades they do. They can simply trade on your recommendations or they can provide you with their investment ideas. Either way, they get paid when you buy and they get paid when you sell.

I don't want anyone to make money simply by making trades in my account. I want someone to get paid based on what choices they make in my account.

Obviously, I think people who try to manage their own money are making a mistake. Actually, I think it's foolhardy. The relative cost of hiring a professional to manage your money can pay for itself many, many times over...if you're working with the right professional.

But how do you really know?

It's All About TRUST

Every part of your relationship with your advisor must be built on trust. Trust is the foundation of the relationship and without it, the relationship is doomed. Trust is what gives you the confidence to know that your advisor is doing the right job whether you're in town, on a vacation, or in the hospital.

Think of it this way: when a broker brings you on as a new client, he or she really doesn't have much to risk. You, on the other hand, are basically saying to that broker, "Here's my money, I really don't know much about you but I'm going to believe in you and trust you will put my money in a high quality portfolio, trust you will make good decisions, trust you will take all things about my particular situation into consideration, and trust you will care not only about me but also my family."

What most people do with their financial planner is rely on the *Blind Trust Principle*. This principle states that unless two people exercise commitment equally in a relationship, one party is at a disadvantage. Or another way of saying it is that one party is giving too much and one party is taking too much. And you as the one with the money are on the wrong side of that equation. So how do you get away from the Blind Trust Principle?

Setting Up Your Expectations

Certainly "trust" is largely a feeling, a confidence, but it can also be established early and maintained through solid business practices. Relationships are a good measuring stick. Often a client thinks more about return than relationship, but the relationship is much more important than most would think. Letting clients know what to expect marks the beginning of a successful relationship. Ongoing and honest communication in writing and in person maintains that relationship.

I have seen so many advisors who seem to "wing" everything: their meetings, their asset management, even their measures of success. This approach can almost work in a thriving market but comes unraveled in a down market. It's the principle so many mortgage companies and banks used in the creation of those countless bad loans. "Why not let people borrow 110% of their home value because the housing prices will go up indefinitely and we'll all be fat and happy."

Ouch, we've seen where that got us.

Giving clients a true sense of meaning and purpose for our services allows them to feel they've received value for the money they've spent. The more we can solidify client expectations, the more value we create. If clients know exactly what I'm doing, why I'm doing it, and how various situations will be handled, they understand the process and are not questioning my value. If they don't understand the process and don't know the strategy, each time the market moves they will question the fee they pay. Sadly, the majority of advisors don't create the atmosphere essential to instilling confidence in their clients.

If an advisor would simply tell clients what he or she will do and when, and then do exactly that, clients would willingly pay double what they would pay someone else. This is the advisor who has created that fundamental trust that will stand the test of both good markets and bad.

Set Your Advisor Free

Trust is also the foundation of something that I believe is key to a successful investor/advisor relationship: freedom. Many brokers will talk to you before they make any transaction in your portfolio. Others will have the authority (which you must give them in writing) to make trades without consulting you.

In a prior life I was a commission broker, and back then I thought that it was always better for the broker to talk to the investor before making a move. This was protection against unethical brokers churning accounts (buying and selling constantly to earn more commissions). What I realized (and this is especially true for fee-based financial managers) is that to be able to do a good job in any decent size firm, the broker must be able to trade without restriction.

A broker needs to be able to get into and out of an investment, not when everyone has signed off on it but when the time is right, using good judgment and expertise to make decisions independently. Giving someone the right to trade your money without you approving every action requires an extraordinary act of trust.

This book is about making certain you put your trust in the right person.

CHAPTER 2

Begin at the Beginning

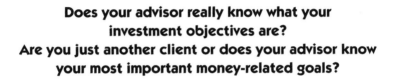

**Does your advisor really know what your
investment objectives are?
Are you just another client or does your advisor know
your most important money-related goals?**

A few years ago a prospect came into my office. She was a single woman, a successful attorney, and she wanted to know when I thought she might be able to retire from her practice. When I asked her why she wanted to retire, she explained that she'd lost her enthusiasm for her work and felt that she wasn't getting the respect she deserved from her male law partners. She was hoping to retire in the next 3–5 years.

I then asked what she wanted to do when she retired. She looked puzzled at first, and said that no one had ever asked her that question before. She started talking about her retirement and quickly warmed up to the subject. It turns out she had an interest in biology and wanted to work with kids and teach them about birds and bugs and all of nature. She wanted to be a volunteer teacher and nature guide.

As we talked, she confessed that part of her motivation to do something else with her life stemmed from the fact that she'd recently lost several family members. Her parents had passed away a couple of years prior and her sister-in-law had suffered a fatal motorcycle accident only a year and a half earlier. She and I both became a little teary eyed as she related the story.

She realized that life was way too short and she didn't want to spend the rest of hers in a law office. She'd also had a recent health scare that made her especially determined to stop wasting time.

After I got all of her financial information, I went to work to figure out a way for her to reach her goals. When she returned to my office for a second meeting, I shared my calculations and a computer print-out showing how she could not only retire soon, she could retire comfortably. She was visibly excited. I then asked her to think about two things before our next meeting: first, how would she want her eulogy to read and second, what exact date would she retire?

When she next returned to my office she could hardly contain herself. Based on the conversations she and I had, she was determined to live the rest of her life to the fullest. She had written and even memorized her eulogy. At her insistence she recited it to me and it was honestly one of the most beautiful eulogies I've ever heard (especially because she was still alive). Finally, she'd met with her partners and set a date to retire in four months. She was inspired.

Of course she became a client and I still meet with her to discuss her account. She's doing great, loving life, doing what she wants to do, and she's never looked back.

If you think that someone's personal goals are no business of their financial advisor, you are dead wrong. To me, knowing what someone wants to really do with their life, even helping them figure it out, is at the heart of what a good advisor should do. How can I plan their investment portfolio well unless I'm clear on what the real objectives are? How can a client suggest their desired level of risk and objectives unless they have a clear target in mind?

Financial planning is most rewarding when I feel I'm participating in the client's greatest aspirations. If your advisor focuses on helping you achieve your goals and dreams, he or she is MUCH more important to you than a broker who's trying to hit a performance number. Advisors who only sell performance are doomed to disappoint their clients because no one's account goes up all the time.

Also, brokers who focus solely on returns are in the commodity business. Commodity businesses compete on price and they'll have to discount their price to get new clients and sometimes to keep current clients. Working with clients to achieve their dreams is literally PRICELESS! An advisor who helps clients meet their goals and realize their dreams will never have his value questioned.

People will pay anything for dreams; they will pay very little for returns unless they are always spectacular.

The Whole Picture

I'm often amazed at how little actual "planning" financial planners really do with their clients. Most often the planning is simply reduced to an investment management plan or a standard financial plan. The advisor never really asks the important questions. And I don't mean the closed-end, one-word answer questions. I mean the touchy feely, thought-provoking questions. The ones that make the hairs on your neck stand up.

I'm talking about questions like this:

- "If you died today, how much and how quickly would you want your kids to inherit your wealth?" (This helps to discover if the client wants his or her kids to value money differently by working for it as opposed to simply inheriting it.)
- "Are any of your children driving cars listed in your name?" (The client should know about potential liability or creditor protection issues.)
- "If you didn't have to work, what would you love to do all day, every day?" (This is another way of determining their true life's passions.)
- "What security measures do you utilize to protect your personal and financial information?" (It's important to be aware of potential identity theft issues.)

My firm came up with a program in 2008 where we began asking our clients these questions and many more. This exercise deepened our client relations significantly. We went from being their Wealth Manager to their True Trusted Advisor. That is the type of interaction every investor should have.

There are so many questions that need to be addressed in order for your advisor to have a complete picture of your situation. But I would venture a guess that less than 5% of financial relationships are anywhere near this comprehensive.

(Visit our website for more of the important questions to consider at www.fireyourbroker.com.)

Facts or Blind Faith?

In truth, a successful broker/client relationship is not easily measured. There's no simple way to measure if your advisor has done a good job. It seems straightforward and reasonable to judge performance based on the rate of return, but this is a subjective measure at best.

Why? Most people compare everything to the S&P 500 Index (500 of the major holdings on the U.S. stock market). While this is an okay measure of the market as a whole, your portfolio should **not** be invested like the S&P because that's a value-weighted index based solely on U.S. companies.

Almost every investor, unless they're totally aggressive, should have some level of fixed income (e.g. bonds) in their portfolio. So basically, when you compare your investment results to the S&P 500, you're comparing apples to oranges. And yet that's how most people evaluate their financial relationship.

So what can you do? In an effort to make the relationship "measurable", your advisor should prepare two documents for you. The first is the *Investment Policy Statement*. This document is filled with information about you. It establishes why you're investing, what kind of risk you're comfortable taking, what your time horizon is, and then the statement connects all of this information to your investment plan.

By following this fundamental information, your advisor will choose investments, make changes to your portfolio, and establish the appropriate investment volatility and expected return. In fairness, no one can accurately predict exactly where the market will go on a day-to-day basis, but this Investment Policy Statement will provide guidelines and expectations over a period of time. It should also give you an excellent sense of what your advisor will do in various situations.

The second document you should expect is the *Financial Policy Statement*. This provides more specific information about your goals for the long term. This document should include when you want to retire, how much money you want to make, other sources of income, and assumed rates of return. In other words, it will summarize your financial plan.

What's sad about the current financial planning environment is that there's typically no real expectation from either planners or investors to have any form of scorecard. The advisor promises to work hard and you keep your fingers crossed. To me, this approach is just wrong. It puts no demands on the advisor and makes one client no different from another.

Every client should be unique. A cookie-cutter approach to investing cheapens the relationship and doesn't serve the individual needs of the client.

The Investment Policy Statement and the Financial Policy Statement are the best ways to know whether you're getting what you're paying for and whether your advisor is following your guidelines. I'd bet the farm that Bernard Madoff didn't provide his clients with these documents.

(For a sample Investment Policy Statement and Financial Policy Statement go to www.fireyourbroker.com.)

A Person or a Number?

An older couple came into the office not long ago to talk about having us manage their money. Around the middle of the meeting after I had already gotten some personal and most of the financial information, I began asking some life-related questions. I said to the wife, "You shared a lot of great things with me today as a couple. But now, I want you to share more things about you in particular. I want you to think about all you've accomplished in life, all of your memories. And out of those memories, I want you to tell me what's missing. What are some of the things that you've wanted to do and just kept putting off, and now you don't know if you'll ever do them?"

She immediately began to tell me that she hated the winters in Northern Virginia. She didn't like the cold and the snow and she absolutely hated the ice storms. She told me that she'd like to live in Florida, if not year round, at least for the winters. But, she knew that her husband would never want to do that.

So I then looked over at the husband. He said he didn't even know that she wanted to live in Florida. He said that he'd be open to spending some time in a warmer climate. He could work from home and it really didn't matter where that home was. And to top it off, he said he'd be happy to move to Florida.

This is a couple that had been married for over 40 years. I'd known them for 45 minutes.

Next I asked the husband if there was anything he'd never accomplished that he'd like to do. And as quickly as I could ask the question, the answer came as a complete surprise to both his wife and me. He said he wanted to skydive! I said, "Skydive?" Now this couple was in their early 70's, a fine age but a time when it's rare for people to take up skydiving.

We talked it through. I told him of my own experience with the sport and in the end, I encouraged him to do it.

The outcome of that meeting was truly amazing. Here was a couple that had dreams and goals inside themselves that their spouse of 40+ years never knew.

And while it took a couple of months, he did skydive (I have the framed picture in my office). And in the first winter following that meeting, they stayed on one of the Bahamian Islands for 3 weeks.

I've shown them how they can retire at least part-time to Florida and they are rejuvenated.

This kind of event happens in my office with regularity. It shows the difference between seeing people as walking accounts and seeing people as individuals, each with unique dreams and aspirations.

Financial Planning is not About a Rate of Return, it's About Achieving Your Goals

Most people think they're in the market to get a specific rate of return, but ironically they typically don't know what that rate should even be. They're so focused on what the market does, they often forget what return they are after. And more importantly, they haven't even done the analysis and planning to determine what they really do need.

First and foremost, your financial future needs some emotion in it. I strongly encourage you to sit down and think about where you want to be in 5, 10, and 20 years. Assemble a list of the things you want to accomplish, where you want to live, what kind of lifestyle you want for yourself and your family, and then start to feel those goals and dreams emotionally. That's where a financial plan really starts.

It's not about the numbers; it's about your life's dreams.

I often ask clients what they have to do to be really happy. Many will say they are happy, but when I dig a little deeper I find there are frequently things they've always wanted to do but haven't. There's still a different kind of person they want to be, something they have to do, some place they have to go. A financial plan starts with uncovering those aspirations and building a financial future around them.

Now this is a business book, not a self-help book. But what I'm about to say is not strictly business. I firmly believe that if you don't seriously think about what you really want to do with your life, vast sums of money won't be very satisfying. Most advisors will be happy to take your money and try to make a significant increase in the principle, but unless you have a target that means something powerful to you personally, it's just numbers.

Do you really care if you have $8 million or $15 million or $40 million in your account? For all intents and purposes the difference, though great, is inconsequential. Only when you relate the money you're making to something meaningful are you personally vested in your investing.

Life goals are extremely important and if your advisor is only focused on whatever return can be squeezed from the market, then both of you are missing the bigger picture. An advisor who knows your most important goals and aspirations is a partner, someone who's almost as emotionally committed to your dreams as you are. This is a partnership that, over the long run, will give you the most outstanding results.

CHAPTER 3

Personal Attention

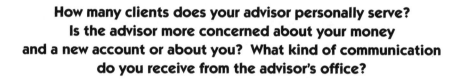

**How many clients does your advisor personally serve?
Is the advisor more concerned about your money
and a new account or about you? What kind of communication
do you receive from the advisor's office?**

I've overheard cynical advisors say, "Financial planning would be a good business if it weren't for the clients." They clearly believe their clients' questions and concerns are more an irritation than an opportunity. This is completely backward. The clients make this profession fun; they become friends. Each client is a world of opportunities.

You need to find an advisor who structures his office, schedule, and business practices to best serve you and all the clients in the firm.

You're looking for an environment that's created to maximize the chances of success on your terms over the long haul. Yes, of course I'm talking about a profitable situation, but profitable for you personally, an environment where the objective is to create a rewarding experience for each client from both a financial and a personal perspective.

You measure this success not just on a one or two year basis but in terms of decades, indeed, the rest of your life…and beyond to the lives of your heirs.

What does this kind of environment look like?

First you need to find out what your advisor's client/planner ratio is. How many clients does each of the representatives in the office serve? The number should be 150 or lower. The more clients a financial representative (or "rep") has, the less time each individual client receives.

Recently I attended a conference of the top 100 wealth managers across America. The lead advisor of a prestigious investment company gave a memorable speech, conveying that his firm was very impressive and did a great job for all their clients. His confidence lasted until he was asked a question by a fellow top 100 planner. The question was, "How many reps do you have and how many clients does the firm have?" The answer was 6 reps and 3000 clients. So when the questioner followed up with, "How can each rep have an average of 500 clients and possibly give them great service?" I remember there was a lot of stumbling with the answer.

So let's do a little math. First, assume there are 2,000 working hours in an average year. If the financial advisor mentioned above meets with each client twice per year with a one-hour appointment each time, that would be exactly half of the advisor's total time (500 clients x 2 hours each = 1,000 total hours). Remember, that same advisor must still plan investment strategy, manage all the accounts, update client information, market to new clients, and participate in continuing education, not to mention vacation days and sick days.

It doesn't sound like the rep is really getting to know each client very well, does it? Is that the kind of relationship you want with a financial planner?

Find an Advisor Who's Selective

You need to determine how committed your advisor is to you. That's relatively easy; how do they conduct themselves in your meetings? Are they giving you ample time to explain your wants and needs? Do they want to hear your story? Do they ask questions about you, your family, your situation, what you're passionate about? The more interested they are in finding out about your whole world, the more interested and committed they'll be in helping you accomplish your goals and dreams. The less interested they are, the more you'll soon feel like you're in the "Returns" line at Wal-Mart.

Go with a planner who won't take just anyone as a client.

A nice couple came into my office a few years ago. They wanted advice on investing their money for retirement. I gave them some general information and while doing so, I assessed whether they would be a good client. They had over $5 million in assets so they were above our account minimum, and they were making several mistakes I knew I could correct. The problem was they, particularly the husband, were know-it-alls.

Each time I started to bring up something they should consider changing, the husband interrupted to inform me he'd tried that but that it didn't work. Normally this would have been okay but it happened every time.

Now I'm pretty easy and don't pretend to always be right, but I know you can't try many financial strategies for a month and know definitively whether or not they work. It was clear to me that arguing with this gentleman would be like arguing with a five-year old. I wasn't going to change his mind.

Several of the questions he asked were really statements designed to show me how knowledgeable he was. It was as if he was trying to prove to his wife that he had a substantial level of knowledge about finances.

At the end of the meeting I inquired if I had answered all of their questions and they agreed that I did. I then told them to have a nice day and began walking them out of my office. They stopped suddenly and said, "Wait a second, aren't you going to schedule another meeting with us or ask if we want to become a client?" With a smile on my face I simply said that they were not a good fit for us. In a polite but candid tone, I told them about how the aim of our firm was to work with people who shared our philosophy of investing. It seemed evident to me that they had their own ideas of investing, which was certainly their prerogative.

But they were not a good client for us, despite their portfolio, and I knew it right away.

At the end of the day, it's not just about trying to get a new client; it's *always* about trying to get the **right** client. That's the kind of planner you want.

Adding a client should always be a two-way selection process. If a firm adds clients regardless of fit, it means either that they have no coherent philosophy of investing or they're willing to sacrifice their mission in the hope of making a few extra dollars. In either case, in that kind of environment everyone suffers.

There is evidence that a good financial advisor can successfully handle only a finite number of relationships. Coincidently, that number is the same as the number of personal relationships an individual can successfully handle; sociologists suggest that the average person can manage no more than 150 associations (this is known as Dunbar's number, based on the studies of psychologist Robin Dunbar in the 1990's). As Dr. Dunbar concluded, beyond this number the connection is not very close.

A real bond between you and your advisor consists of several contacts throughout a year. It's extremely important to feel that you've established a bond with your financial manager that includes regular personal communication. I'm not talking about just a single meeting each year but the type of relationship that encourages you to call when you have questions.

When you call the office, you should feel welcomed and appreciated whether you speak directly to your advisor or not. This kind of reception can only happen in an office that's properly structured and one with the right number and kind of clients.

A Team Approach

It may at first seem like a contradiction, but I believe that the client and the firm are best served by a team approach. It's often not necessary to talk directly to your advisor each time you have a basic question. Most questions can be answered quickly and effectively by a staff member, freeing up the advisor to concentrate on the most important aspects of the job like making investment decisions and holding face-to-face meetings with clients.

The standard financial planning office is set up with two main people, the advisor and one assistant. For the advisor who has a great business sense, this can work. A majority of advisors, however, aren't strong in the structure and operation of a business. The usual issue for the advisor who's not a businessperson is that he or she doesn't realize the inherent flaw in trying to be all things to all people.

This approach creates problems exponentially as the office adds clients. The advisor is jumping from taking calls about someone's account, to meeting with a new client over allocating their portfolio, to meeting with someone who was referred to the firm by another client, to watching the market for the right moment to make a trade, to talking to his assistant about her annual review…all before lunch.

So with that kind of operation, how high do you think you rate on that advisor's radar screen? If you're only a high priority at the moment you call, that's a reactive planner, not a proactive one. You want a planner who is forward thinking and who is a step or two ahead of the growth curve, not constantly trying to catch up with growth.

The ideal office will have a set up that is quite different from what I've just described. The advisor will have not only financial acumen but also business sense. In other words, he or she will know how to secure business by doing the best job from a strict financial planning standpoint, but will also be able to keep clients by offering great service. Those two abilities require very different skill sets.

The best office will have an advisor who realizes that it's critical to budget time carefully. There will be several administrative staff members, including the Director of First Impressions (receptionist) who answers the phone and greets everyone as they come in the door. The Fire Marshal (customer relations specialist) is the one assisting customers who call with a specific issue. The job is to "put out the fire." A majority of calls routed to this person involve a clerical issue but the individual in this position will likely have a financial background as the questions can often relate to investment topics.

Beyond these two critical staff people, an advisor may have one or more administrative assistants who know all the advisor's clients and are familiar with their portfolios. The larger financial managers may even have researchers who are responsible for studying and making recommendations on various types of investments. Some managers will hire financial planners responsible for coordinating and inputting data for client financial plans.

Some of the best offices will even have an accountant, an attorney, a life insurance specialist, mortgage broker, and possibly a health insurance expert either on staff or have an affiliation set up to be able to refer and consult with these professionals.

Time Really is Money

Your time is valuable and your advisor's time is too. How advisors set up and run meetings are good indicators of how much they value your time *and* their own. The best consultants will have a significant monetary value attached to their time. They realize that time is *the* most limited commodity.

It's so important to work with people who are busy. There's a cliché in business, find a busy person and ask them to do something and it WILL get done, period. They are not the ones with time to hang out at the water cooler; they don't have time to chit-chat. They realize they have things to get done and only a limited amount of time. They are typically good delegators who surrounded themselves with professionals. They quickly find the best person for each job and pass some of the responsibility on. They are organized and methodical but also recognize their own weaknesses and have ways to compensate for the things they don't do well.

Effective managers know they're not perfect and the smart ones have "tricks" or habits that make these imperfections imperceptible. They will use things like having a clock in their line of view so they can start and end meetings on time. They will have agendas for each meeting so that nothing is left on the table. You may not even notice some of the behind-the-scenes tools they use to keep themselves on track.

After each meeting the successful advisor will have some kind of note-taking program or dictation service so that they can transcribe notes from the meeting. At the end of those notes, there will be a "to do" list that will be given to those in the office who need to follow up. This is the epitome of efficiency. It also provides a great record from each meeting about what was said and done and what has yet to be done. Before the next meeting with the same client, it's easy for anyone in the office to monitor what progress has been made.

Think of a well-run doctor's office. You sign in, fill out some paperwork, sit and wait. When you're called to the examination area, the nurse will get your vitals and ask the reason for your visit. When the doctor arrives he or she has already looked at the file from your last appointment, knows why you're there, and gives you about 15 minutes of time to figure out your situation and remedy. Someone else then usually performs that remedy.

Plain and simple, the doctor's time is very valuable so it makes no sense for the doctor to take your blood pressure. That time is better spent in diagnosing the problem and prescribing a solution. Everything else is done by a staff member who's lower on the payroll. If your doctor was taking your height and weight, the cost of your health insurance would probably be astronomical.

Think of your financial advisor as a doctor. If your advisor truly is as good as you hope, then his or her time is of the highest value. Your advisor should be listening to you describe your pain and then prescribing what to do to fix your concern.

Someone else is taking the data, inputting information into the computer, printing statements, and perhaps even looking at your tax returns. The financial situation is then summarized for the advisor who can spend more time listening to you and explaining what will help your situation. The best advisors understand this.

Unfortunately, many people in the financial world consider themselves artists instead of business people. Financial planning is still a business and the larger a firm gets, the more systems and tools must be in place to properly handle client accounts and management.

You want to work with an office that's run very efficiently. The ones that aren't may not be around for very long or will constantly go through growing pains which are certain to have a negative impact on your account.

What should also be clear is the almost insurmountable challenge a one or two person firm faces in having to perform every function. Without a staff, it's the advisor who's wasting time on menial tasks that take away from the critical aspects of the job.

Similarly, there are investors who are upset if they can't speak directly to their advisor every time they call. Some of these investors have large sums of money at risk and assume that they should receive impeccable service. I agree they should receive great service, every investor should, but if the advisor is taking calls that a staff member can answer then everyone suffers.

The bottom line is that you're looking for an investment firm that's professional and efficient. This typically means it's large enough that the advisor can focus on what's important and not so large that your advisor couldn't pick you out of a lineup.

Perhaps a simpler way to tell if your advisor sees you as a person or a number is in the communication you receive from the office.

Who Makes the Calls?

Does your broker consistently call you when it's time to meet? Does he or she keep you informed by providing regular communication? When it comes to your money and the relationship with your financial advisor, communication is a MUST. Many broker/client relationships are built on the client making the first call to the broker when there are questions or concerns. I've heard so many stories about someone who called their broker expecting a call back that day and waiting in vain for the phone to ring.

And it didn't ring...not that day, not the next day. In some cases the broker called back over a week later and other times never called back at all.

Communication is so crucial to the relationship that without it there is no real relationship.

Here's the key about communication: you shouldn't always initiate it. The best planners will have call rotation schedules for each client's account review.

This review should happen *at least* once a year. As a matter of fact, if your broker is charging a fee for advisory services, then that advisor has a legal, fiduciary obligation to have a face-to-face meeting with you at least once a year.

I'm always amazed when a prospective client tells me, "My broker hasn't contacted me in over a year. Anytime I want something, I have to call him."

If that's the case, it's simple, get a new broker. Always remember you hired that person to do a job for you; you gave them the keys to your financial future, your life's savings. And they can't find the time to even call you? That's absurd. And if they're only calling you to pitch their latest stock recommendation, that's even worse.

In late 2008 when the media was having their frenzy about the market, you couldn't turn on a TV or open a newspaper without seeing or hearing bad news. Our clients were scared, everyone was. So as a benefit for our clients, we sent out an email each time the market had a frightening move in order to explain what was going on and why.

We also invited all of our clients and their friends to a number of "town hall" meetings where my Chief Investment Officer, an outside expert, and I sat at the front of a large auditorium and led a discussion about the markets. We answered any and all of our clients' questions. We knew we couldn't change the markets but at least we could explain to our clients what was happening. During the most turbulent times, we called all of our clients and met with most of them in person.

That is what I mean about clear open communication. Your broker initiates it, it's timely, and it's important to your peace of mind. You should expect it, because you're paying for it.

Soliciting Client Feedback

An advisor who is interested in clients' opinions is an advisor who understands the definition of "service." Most advisors would prefer to not hear what their clients think because they fear that their methods will be questioned.

During challenging times, "That's the way we've always done it" is not a good explanation for why an office operates a particular way. In my opinion tough times are the best time to seek the input and guidance of people whose thoughts and observations really matter: our clients.

It may seem trivial to ask clients about the correspondence they receive, whether they prefer email or snail mail, or how they like the content or frequency of their management meetings, or even what types of refreshments they prefer at meetings. But the answers to these questions are extremely important to enhancing the overall client experience.

Very few brokers ask questions. They feel that they know how to run their practice and don't need to poll their audience. Most often I think brokers don't solicit opinions because they're afraid to hear the truth.

It's actually quite easy to ask for input from clients and it can be done in one of two ways. First, your advisor can send out *client surveys*. These questionnaires can cover a world of information. The only problem is that clients have to actually read and complete them. This is often easier said than done.

Nowadays with all of the great Internet options it's very easy to put out a survey using email tools like Survey Monkey or Zoomerang. These programs allow your advisor to put together a list of questions with multiple-choice answers and send it out via email. These surveys are not only easy to distribute, but easy for the clients to complete.

If you are fortunate enough to have an advisor who sends you a survey, please respond. The survey is a sincere attempt to enhance your investing experience.

There is another way to ask for help from clients and it's a way we've tried to proactively enhance our clients' experiences with my firm. We have a *Client Advisory Board.*

Once a year we ask a number of clients to meet with us on a Saturday morning so we can solicit their opinions about our operation. At this meeting we ask this select group (ideally a good mix of people of different backgrounds, ages, and net-worths) what they think about every area of our business.

We ask the group about our client service, our account performance, what they think about the start-up process when they first became a client. We even ask if there's anything they absolutely hate. And the scary part about this whole process is that we tell them that it's a "no holds barred" process, meaning they can say **anything** about any part of our practice and we will view it as constructive. And believe me; my clients have been brutally honest.

Think about it, wouldn't it be great to have a forum where you could let your advisor know what you like and dislike about the operation?

At one of our Advisory Board meetings, we found out that our clients didn't feel we needed to have status meetings four times a year. They said not much typically changes in that short a time-frame and to meet each quarter was really overkill. So we immediately sent out a letter telling all our clients that after researching the timing of our meetings, we were going to begin meeting only twice per year. Those who still wanted to meet every three months were welcome to continue on the old schedule.

Interestingly enough, we immediately began getting emails from clients saying they were happy we decided to change. Almost everyone thought four meetings were too much. We only had a handful that said they wanted to continue quarterly meetings.

There is so much great information to be gained by simply asking questions. Setting up the environment to receive that information is one of the most important things your advisor can do. It's a clear sign that your advisor actually cares about you and cares about doing the best job possible.

Get it in Writing

In American business every serious financial transaction is done with a contract, except financial planning. Think about it. If you buy a house, car, nice jewelry, a boat, they're all purchased with a contract outlining exactly what you're buying and under what conditions. The terms of the deal, the guarantee and warrantees are all stated clearly in ink. But in the financial services industry most relationships aren't based on a written document but more on verbal points that can't ever be proven or quantified. Seems odd, doesn't it?

Think about your house. The average house across the country is valued at around $200,000 based on a recent study (yes, that average number is falling). Compare that figure to the actual value of your investments throughout your life. Many investors have accounts of $1,000,000 to as much as $5,000,000 or more. Your investments can have so much more value than your home, yet you hire someone to look after those investments without having a contract or anything in writing. But the fault isn't yours.

When it comes to investing, advisors are afraid to put things in writing, and to a certain extent you can't blame them. With all of the lawsuits and arbitration proceedings, it's no wonder the investment community has shied away from contracts. But as a client you're inherently taking a risk. So why shouldn't you get something in writing?

Many brokers are restricted by what their broker/dealer will allow them to do and say. A broker/dealer is a sponsoring company like a franchisor. Coldwell Banker allows individual brokers to operate as a Coldwell Banker real estate franchise if they pay a fee and operate to company standards. Financial broker/dealers are "brand name" firms like Fidelity, Morgan Stanley, and Merrill Lynch in addition to independent firms such as LPL Financial, Commonwealth Financial Network, and Raymond James Financial.

In the financial industry a broker/dealer arrangement allows a broker to get licensed with the Financial Industry Regulatory Agency (FINRA) and/or the Securities and Exchange Commission (SEC). Through the broker/dealer your local broker can obtain a license in the various states where he conducts business and trades on the market, as well as provide a way for the advisor to get paid for the work he does.

As in the real estate industry, a broker/dealer is like the back office of a real estate broker. Because there is this kind of partnership, why does the broker/dealer restrict what their advisors can say? First of all, most broker/dealers have several hundred to several thousand representatives. All of these reps come from different backgrounds and have different experiences. With such a variety of people in play, the broker/dealer has to limit what is put in writing. From a liability standpoint they can't let their reps use their own contracts, as this would be almost impossible to manage. Having a contract for all of their advisors would create a document so general and innocuous that it would be useless.

FINRA also has strict rules as to what actually can be put in writing, as written statements could easily be misleading. Limiting what can be put in writing alleviates the fears of the broker/dealer as well as satisfying the FINRA rules.

Nevertheless, I still believe the best planning is done by putting things in writing, as in the case of the Investment Policy Statement and the Financial Policy Statement.

Why would you want to have these documents in place? Both the Investment and the Financial Policy Statement provide accountability. They set the "rules of engagement" and become a kind of owner's manual. You need to know what your advisor expects from you and what you should expect from your advisor.

To me it's very helpful to have some way to grade an advisor's overall performance. And I am not just talking about rate of return. I'm talking about service and the degree to which they help you accomplish your goals. The Financial Policy Statement is a reminder of why you hired your advisor in the first place and a measure of how well your plan is working.

Imagine this…you are called by your financial advisor's office to come in for your semi-annual review. You establish a time and in about a week, you receive a letter confirming your appointment. You arrive at the rep's office and are greeted by a wonderful Director of First Impressions who offers you a variety of drinks and snacks. Within a few minutes you're invited back to your advisor's office to begin your meeting.

After some initial greetings, the rep pulls out an agenda detailing exactly what will be covered during the meeting. The main focus of the meeting begins with the Financial Policy Statement to see if anything has changed and then the focus turns to whether you are or aren't on track with the goals initially established in the Financial Policy Statement.

Next, the Investment Policy Statement comes out and both the investment mix and performance are reviewed. The advisor shows how he or she is adhering to the Statement and asks if everything is still current. You ask questions and should get direct answers. At the end of the meeting, the rep ends on time with a final greeting and you're on your merry way feeling good about how your life's savings are being handled.

Does that sound too good to be true? Well that's the way every meeting at your advisor's office should work. You leave knowing that you got what you paid for based on real, written expectations. Accountability is key and the best financial advisors aren't afraid of it, they welcome it.

CHAPTER 4

Dart Thrower

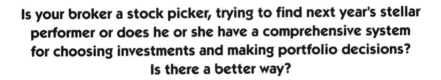

Is your broker a stock picker, trying to find next year's stellar performer or does he or she have a comprehensive system for choosing investments and making portfolio decisions? Is there a better way?

There's a famous story that was once popular among investors. It involves an experiment in which a monkey's ability to pick stocks was measured against the best efforts of several notable stockbrokers. The monkey was given a handful of darts and placed in front of the stock report pages from the newspaper. The monkey fired the darts at the pages and whatever stocks were hit became the monkey's portfolio. The experts picked an equal number of "winners" using their best analysis. After six months the monkey reportedly had selected the best performing investments. I don't know if the story is true but it pretty well captures my opinion of stock pickers.

Stock picking is from the age of dinosaurs. In order to profit by picking the right stock your broker has to make two correct decisions. One is when to buy that miracle company at its market low and the other is when to sell it at the peak. I mean no disrespect to the brokerage industry, but those two decisions are so difficult that to accomplish either with any consistency is almost impossible. Yet many financial advisors use stock picking as a primary investment strategy.

So why, you ask, do mutual fund managers seem to live and die by stock picking? Managers of credible funds have their own experience to draw upon, but they also have their team of analysts and researchers that look at corporate information and buying opportunities all day, every day. Many fund managers will have sophisticated computer systems that analyze the market, historical information about each company, and myriads of factual and statistical information that enable them to make buying and selling decisions. And still, the majority of these funds don't outperform the market.

It makes no sense that individual brokers without these resources strive to be stock pickers. Years ago before any of our sophisticated computer programs even existed, advisors were stock pickers. That was a time when investment information was not readily available through the Internet, and business networks like CNBC didn't even exist. It was a time when there was a significant information gap between when something happened and when everyone actually knew about it. You could find out some key information about a company before most people and then make an investment decision based on that information…often at a profit. Those were simpler times.

Now, information is so readily available that you can go online and listen to an analyst discuss the latest information from any company, national or international, at any time. That's the information age. And this age has taken away many of the former opportunities in the market. Nevertheless many brokers still aspire to be stock pickers because that's the way they used to do it or that's what their mentors taught them. And those brokers have not changed with the times.

In a January, 2009 article in *USA Today*, John Waggoner investigated the phenomenon of "market timers", aka stock pickers. He cites the work of Arch Crawford "The nation's top timer last year," who makes his market decisions using a combination of "technical analysis—and astrology."

Crawford says, "Sometimes the astrology is very significant, and a lot of other times it's not." Crawford had one good year but over the last ten, he lost an average of 1% per year.

Waggoner goes on to say, "Academics say there's little evidence that any market-timing system will work over the long term, and that any top-performing timer is simply a fluke. Your biggest danger with a timer: you'll get a set of bad calls that leaves you selling low and buying high." Somehow that doesn't sound enticing to me no matter how Mars and Venus line up.

It's not unusual for a broker to find a stock that goes up 100% or more. But this is almost always in conjunction with finding others that go nowhere and still more that lose all of their value…making the overall portfolio return dismal.

Unsophisticated investors are nevertheless attracted to stock picking. Many want individual stocks in their portfolio because it's investing they can understand and because of the tax treatment of those securities.

When you own a stock, you're only taxed on a stock's growth when you sell it. Let's say you buy stock A at $10/share and a year later that stock is worth $12/share. So now you've made a 20% return, but unless you sell stock A, you don't have to pay any tax. It's not the same for a mutual fund. A mutual fund going from $10/share to $12/share could be taxable to you whether you sell or not. It all depends on whether the fund manager sold any of the underlying holdings to achieve that return. If so, you'd have a tax liability.

Investors are attracted to stocks for their tax efficiency but dislike them because they're not diversified. Conversely, they like mutual funds for the diversification but don't like them because they're not tax efficient. There must be something better.

Better Options

There is a way to get the best of both worlds, to have the tax advantage of individual stocks and the lower risk of a mutual fund; it's called an Exchange Traded Fund (ETF). ETFs are diversified like mutual funds in that they're pooled investments with set criteria on how the investments are chosen (for example you could have an Index ETF that follows a certain type of index.)

ETFs can be more efficient than mutual funds in that they trade like a stock. When a stock is purchased, it's purchased at a specific moment at a specific price. ETFs share that same process. Mutual funds trade at the end of the day based on the price at the close of the market.

Also when one stock in an ETF is sold and another purchased, the transaction is handled as a *like-kind exchange*. Due to the tax efficient rules of like-kind exchanges, your gain from the stock being sold, if any, is transferred to the stock being purchased. In effect you're deferring the tax that would otherwise be payable in the same mutual fund transaction. Just like an individual stock.

Another efficiency with ETFs is that they usually have a lower internal expense ratio than their mutual fund counterpart. There is typically not an active manager to pay so the cost can be lower.

The ultimate question is: does your broker pick individual stocks or does he or she do additional research to come up with potentially more efficient investment options? In an ever-changing global investment world, a capable advisor needs to be aware of everything out there and determine which strategies can most help your portfolio.

There is one additional condemnation of stock picking I need to mention. Brokers and individual investors may be successful in purchasing one or two winning stocks, but then they frequently don't know when to sell. Remember, buy low and sell high. But often, winners are never sold. Even if an investor said they want to hold onto their "winners", they should at least sell a portion of those stocks when they're at a high.

Rebalancing Pays Off Long-Term

Rebalancing is the process of keeping your portfolio allocation stable over time. When you have long-term investments, you should look at their relative value in comparison to the overall portfolio. If one of your investments is supposed to be 20% of the portfolio and now is 30%, rebalancing would require you to sell a portion of that investment. The proceeds from that sale would be used to buy more of one of the categories of investments in the portfolio that is at too low a percentage.

For the most part, rebalancing follows the principle of buying low and selling high, without being greedy. I refer you to that famous Wall Street maxim, "Bulls make money, bears make money, pigs get slaughtered."

Here's an example why rebalancing can be critical. Many people's portfolios got completely out of balance during the "tech boom" of 1995–1999. And because of this imbalance, they fully participated in the "tech bust" of 2000–2002.

John (I never use real names of clients) and I first met in 1996. He came to me from a workshop I'd given on Asset Allocation. After the workshop, he asked if he could bring in his portfolio for my review. At our meeting, I saw that he had done very well in a couple of technology stocks. As a matter of fact, those stocks brought him a return of over 50% each and had become a substantial part of his portfolio.

Instead of taking some of his winnings off the table, in the euphoria of those boom years, John decided to let things ride. Those two tech stocks represented about 10% of his portfolio at the beginning of 1996, and by the end of the year the tech positions now represented nearly 25% of his plan. I strongly advised John that his portfolio was badly out of balance.

I didn't accept John as a client because his ideas about investing and mine were not compatible. He ignored my advice for the next couple of years, but kept in touch. He continued to allow these two tech stocks to grow without worrying about what a substantial percentage of his account they had become. Near the end of 1999, I saw his portfolio and those two positions represented about 85% of his investments. I remember having a conversation with him specifically about how he should sell some of those two positions because the technology sector was way over-valued.

He asked why he should sell any of those two high-performing investments to purchase something else which stood to be inferior. And to boot, why pay the long-term capital gains tax on the sale of those holdings?

I simply told him that too much of a good thing is always a problem at some point. He refused to listen. After the market went down beginning in March of 2000, I wondered if I would hear from him again. I didn't until almost a year later. I was conducting another workshop in Northern Virginia and saw John in the audience. After the program, he said, "I really wish you would have been pushier about selling those two tech stocks."

I was afraid to ask the question but did, "What happened to them, John?" He said both companies continued to rise in the first months of 2000, even after the fall of the market. But later in the year both stocks had significant issues. One ended up having reporting irregularities (meaning their balance sheet had been portrayed as better than it actually was) and the other had several venture funds backing it and when the funds bailed out, the company couldn't make payroll. All in all, both stocks ended up being worthless within a few months. John was distraught, but it was his own fault. He let greed control his portfolio rather than having a disciplined system of investing. I couldn't bring myself to say, "I told you so."

Had he listened to my advice, he would have earmarked a certain amount of money for the tech sector in his portfolio. When that position became overvalued by perhaps 20%, we would have sold *some* of it and purchased another position in the portfolio that was not performing as well. This is the essence of the "buy low sell high" philosophy.

With the amount of money that John made *on paper* through 1997–1998, he should have rebalanced several times. Had he done that, he'd now have the option to retire and never have to think about work again. Instead, he chose to follow the road most traveled and ride the wave all the way up… then all the way down. John unfortunately has many more years before he can retire, simply because he got greedy.

Discipline is the hallmark of a successful investor. The easiest way to insure discipline is to have a system in place that tells you what to trade and when. There's little guesswork, no indecision, no emotion, only the numbers dictating when a trade should be made. It's the only way to invest.

Strict Investment Rules Work the Best

Don't choose an investment manager who lets you make all of the decisions. What's the point of having an investment manager if you're making the trades? It's cheaper to just do it yourself. If your investment manager caves in when the market crashes that simply means he or she didn't have a strong investment philosophy.

A structured approach to investing is essential for most advisors. Advisors commonly see themselves as market analysts when in fact they are really marketers. Truth be told, many of them spend far more time farming for new clients than they do studying the markets. This split focus can almost work if they have a disciplined investing system, otherwise they have to be watching the markets constantly…which they can't and won't do. A structured system is basically a framework of "rules" for buying and selling.

Here are some examples of rules that work. When the profit on an investment is greater than an established percentage of the investment, sell at least 50% of your gain. Once you've made 100% return, take out all of your original principle.

Other rules determine when to sell a loser. For instance, holding on to an investment because you're waiting for it to come back is often ludicrous, but that's what most people do. Think of it as being in a sinking boat and not jumping out before it goes under water. I hope you're a good swimmer if this is your approach.

A good sell rule is to get out of any investment when it's lost 25% of its purchase price. This sounds difficult but most investment companies will allow you to use *stop loss* orders. This order creates a standing rule that you want to "automatically" sell a certain investment when it goes down by 25%. The computer will place a "sell" order if the prescribed fall occurs. Updating this order is important, especially in a volatile market. If the market goes up considerably, your advisor may want to adjust your order to reflect that up-swing. Conversely, if the asset class as a whole goes down or the market has a really bad day, you may not want to sell. In that case your advisor simply adjusts the order. Your investment manager may only have the computer issue an alert if the stock drops the established percentage. A decision can then be made whether to execute the trade based on current market conditions. Don't try that at home.

Also, don't let the tax tail wag the investment dog. Many investment managers will let clients make decisions purely on tax considerations. Time and time again I've seen situations where someone holds on to an investment for months, even years, due to the tax obligation they'd have if they sold it.

During the tech boom, investors would hold very profitable stocks waiting for the investment to go from "short term" to "long term" capital gains. Or they'd wait until next year when their tax rate would potentially be lower. But by then the market had turned sour. They ended up not paying any tax at all because their investment had gone belly up. Let taxes be a consideration but don't let them be your sole decision criterion.

The best financial advisor will have a system for all investment planning and buy/sell decisions. The best financial advisor will be the one who realizes that stock picking is better left to the professional money manager or done with a systematic approach such as indexing…or not done at all.

A Smarter Way to Invest

We all remember Enron, that company where many employees lost virtually everything they had simply because they bought company stock. But was the dramatic loss because they bought company stock…or was it because that stock was such a large portion of each employee's net worth?

Choosing *pooled* investments is a better approach. These types of investments involve investing in a group of companies, bought and sold as a package, such as mutual funds or Exchange Traded Funds. They tend to be less volatile and thus more predictable. You won't likely double your money in six months but you probably won't lose it all either.

If you're looking at mutual funds make sure your broker is very selective, as many funds don't beat their relative index and many are not very tax efficient. As a rule of thumb, 50–80% of the mutual funds do not beat their associated index. This means that most growth and income mutual funds **do not** perform better than the S&P 500 Index. Depending on the market conditions, even more than 80% don't beat the index.

The bottom-line question becomes, "Why should I invest in an actively managed mutual fund when statistically the fund most likely won't out-perform its own index. Why wouldn't I just buy the *index fund?*" And that's a great question.

An index fund is an investment in any one of the broader financial groups of stocks, bonds, etc., such as the S&P 500, the entire NASDAQ, or in any of the stock markets around the world. An index fund generally has a lower cost which automatically tends to make it a better investment choice.

The real issue in choosing to invest in mutual funds comes down to how much money you can spend on analysis tools, and on what types of funds you will be able to purchase depending on what brokerage company you utilize (not all investment companies can invest in every kind of mutual fund).

If your advisor has the knowledge, is willing to pay for the analysis tools, and can work with the institutional funds, he or she will likely outperform the market and be able to consistently choose the best funds.

One of the best ways to choose top-performing funds is to use a tool like Morningstar Principia. This is a program that will cost $1,000 – $2,000 per year for the full analysis capability. The website allows you to do a search of all the funds that are top-rated in their category for the last one, three, and five year periods and beyond. You'll have the ability to see which managers have consistently outperformed their index. You'll also see those funds that are one or two year sensations but are not consistently good performers. You'll be able to find funds and fund managers that outperform their peers and indices each and every year. There's a famous saying that "past performance is not indicative of future returns," but the fact is, consistency **is** the best measure of competence and the best bet for future returns.

Clearly mutual funds have some inherent drawbacks. Exchange Traded Funds are, for my money, a much better alternative. ETFs are like mutual funds in that they are pooled investments. Exchange Traded Funds can be more tax efficient than mutual funds and *enhanced indexing* techniques utilized by some ETF companies can out-perform the index more consistently.

When dealing with Exchange Traded Funds, we try to out-perform the index not just mirror the index. There are ways to accomplish exactly that. A major shift in the ETF world came about with enhanced indexing. This process works by taking an index and then adding "filtering" criteria that will limit the number of stocks in the pool. For example, to enhance the S&P 500 Index we could first use an equal weighting giving each stock 1/500th of the value of the portfolio. Now we set some additional criteria, such as eliminating the worst 200 stocks from the index, and keep only those stocks with rising annual dividends in the last 3 years.

Each time we add more criteria, we enhance the quality of the stocks remaining in the index. It's been shown that 90–95% of the actively managed mutual funds **do not** beat enhanced indexing. It would be almost impossible to always find the top 5–10% of the funds on the market due to annual fluctuations. So if we can continually search for ETFs that are based on enhanced indexing, we will have some of the best pooled investments available.

Asset Allocation Works

Market timing does not work, but *asset allocation* does. If you're in a down market, a panicked reaction of many individuals and financial managers is to sell everything and go to cash. The problem is that this is another form of stock picking or market timing. Making that type of decision again requires you to be correct twice.

First, you need to be able to sell at the right time (when the market is still at a high) and second, you need to be able to get back into the market at the right time (when the market is at a low). Most individual investors, brokers, wealth managers and fund managers can't make either one of those decisions correctly. How can you expect to make both at the right time?

So what should your broker be doing? Well first of all, the answer is not simple but it's easier than one would think.

The word you need to understand when investing is *correlation*. Correlation is the key to building an investment portfolio. The easiest way to understand correlation is to imagine the colors of the rainbow. You remember ROYGBIV: red, orange, yellow, green, blue, indigo and violet. Picture each color as a separate kind of investment. Each is very individualized, very distinct. They all have their own position in the spectrum but don't look at all like one another. Together they form a beautiful pattern, in investment terms, a complete portfolio.

Most people (and many advisors) have a portfolio with just one color, like reds. They may have bright red, maroon, pink and hot pink. All are distinct but all are in the same family. A portfolio in these shades may seem diversified, but it still contains all similar positions. Other people don't have just reds, they may have many shades of red, a couple of variations of yellow and a blue. While that's more diversified, it still doesn't contain the full spectrum of investments.

What if I could add ALL the colors of the rainbow to my portfolio? Think how diversified that would be. The more colors I add, especially distinct ones, the more diversification I have, the lower my risk, and the more consistent my return.

The point of this colorful analogy is that diversification is key to long-term success in the investment world. A majority of investors and money managers have favorite categories of investments with which they are familiar and that give them a feeling of comfort.

This is false security. If you're invested only in the red spectrum and the reds get clobbered, you're in big trouble. It's like being overinvested in tech stocks before that sector of the market turned toxic.

In simplest terms, correlation is the science of how different categories of investments move in relation to each other. Using correlation in investing is selecting the mix of investment categories that won't all move in the same direction at the same time.

A couple of years ago I met with a prospective client who was referred by our CPA. This gentleman was only in his forties but was very successful in his business and had no debt, I mean none.

When we began to review his portfolio, I saw something that was an all too familiar sight. He has 92 holdings broken down into seven different accounts. Five of the accounts could have been combined into one but that wasn't the real problem. When I looked at the 92 individual securities and reviewed the allocation in our portfolio software, I found that his investments were completely out of balance.

He was greatly over-invested in large companies that were value-oriented. What I mean was that he had all of his investments in "blue chip" type stocks. In other words, he had all reds in his portfolio but not the rest of the rainbow. It was almost like his broker was trying to create his own mutual fund.

So what's the problem with this type of allocation? It may sound like nice conservative investing and if the market is doing well, there is nothing wrong. But when the market is going south, especially for the large cap, value asset class, then his entire portfolio will do poorly. All of his holdings will tend to react the same way to the movement of the overall market.

The man soon became a client and we were able to add many more colors to his investment spectrum. We reduced his risk and even gave him a better return. And we were able to show him the improvement because we compared his old portfolio to the new one after two years. His return had increased by 11%, which was a substantial amount of money given the size of his investment.

You don't want a portfolio in which every investment reacts similarly to whatever market conditions come along. You want some that tend to go one way and some that tend to react opposite. Done well, diverse investments complement each other and flow together like the colors of a rainbow.

Another way to understand correlation is to think about body builders. Now I'm a workout fanatic but am in no way a body builder (ask my wife). But what would happen if I went to the gym everyday and worked only on my biceps? After a time I might have big biceps but I'd look ridiculous, completely out of balance. What's more, without developing the correlating arm muscles, my arms would fail to function effectively. The best body builders seek to develop all muscles in proportion. Those are the folks who win the trophies.

So it is with portfolios, the strongest portfolios are in balance and proportion with no one investment category dominating the others.

Adding a little investment flexibility is also a key. Most people, including mutual fund managers, buy an investment on the premise that the market will go up and so will that investment. This frequently works. The problem is that most market cycles are historically four to six years long. For simplicity, assume a four year cycle. In that cycle the market typically increases three of those years and decreases in one. So you're making money 75% of the time and losing money 25% of the time. This is the way most of the world invests. Remember though, if we do the same thing everyone does, we'll get the same results everyone gets.

So what should we do differently? First we give our investment managers some flexibility. We might include some investments that can make money even if the market goes down. That way we're at least partially covered regardless of which way the market moves.

Here's how it works. When you buy a stock, you buy it to hold "long". That means if the stock price goes up you make money, and if the stock price goes down you lose money. If we simply change our philosophy to allow our manager to sell "short" the opposite happens.

Participating in a short investment means that you do some fancy borrowing of stock so that if the price goes down you make money, and if the price goes up you actually lose money. This basic flexibility of long and short investing can do two major things. It allows you to not lose as much money if the market goes down, and it also allows your advisor to choose investments on both sides of the risk balance sheet, ones he thinks will go up and ones he thinks will go down.

We're not betting against ourselves but hoping to gain on both winners and losers. Well over 95% of investors do not understand this investment strategy, so they do not use it in their portfolios.

The best security in the volatile, historically unpredictable world of investing is a wide and carefully selected mix of investments from a divergent range of categories, categories sometimes outside the domestic arena.

A Global World Requires a Global Investment Mix

The exponential growth of the Internet combined with the frenetic expansion of economies in countries like China, India, and Brazil has redefined the way business is done in the world. The days when America was the sole dominant player in the business world are long gone. Rather than lament that change, we should embrace it and adapt our strategies to reflect the new environment.

Because the business world has shifted to a global market, you must have *global asset allocation*. We all know companies like McDonalds, headquartered in the U.S., but with operations all over the globe. Virtually all major American companies have significant operations in other countries.

Similarly, the largest companies based elsewhere around the world all have, or are trying to have, business operations in the U.S. Given this reality, wouldn't it make sense to change your investment allocations from a mainly domestic focus to more of a global approach? It's pretty obvious isn't it?

We know that the more asset classes we add to a portfolio, the lower the risk and the more consistent the return. By thinking more globally we can add many, many more asset classes to our mix, lowering the risk even further.

"But wait," you say, "it seems like when the market goes strongly up or down in the U.S., the other stock markets around the world follow suit. What good does going global do in that scenario?"

The answer is simple: you should not be invested in **just** stocks, here or around the world.

What's important is the mix of investments. For example, take an initial portfolio of Large, Mid and Small Cap Stocks, Government Bonds, Corporate Bonds, and Real Estate, all from the U.S. Most investors will simply add an International Stock Fund and call it done. But now let's add Global Real Estate, Global Currencies, Global Commodities and Global Fixed Income for starters. With those added categories diversification has markedly increased and your risk is almost cut in half.

Interestingly enough you'd think with much less risk, you'd have decreased your return proportionally. Well, that simply is not the case. As a matter of fact, you actually lowered your risk and increased your return for both the short term and the long term. That's the power of global asset allocation that most brokers and investors do not understand.

All of these investing specifics are a long-winded way of making sure you understand that there are many, many investing strategies that make a whole lot more sense than stock picking. You or your advisor can certainly stand shoulder to shoulder with the monkey and fling darts at a chart, but know that there are smarter, safer, and more consistently winning approaches out there.

CHAPTER 5

Less Is Not More

Does your advisor have account minimums or will he or she work with anyone who walks through the door?

When I first began in the financial services industry in 1991, I started by selling life insurance as many in our industry do. I was pretty good at it and quickly ended up with a lot of clients. I was definitely not picky about whom I accepted as a client. If you had a heartbeat you could be my client. If you wanted life insurance, you just needed a decent heartbeat. I had no account minimums.

I remember working with a husband and wife who both needed life insurance policies. I was all excited when they agreed to purchase two policies for a total of $50/month. I called my girlfriend (now my wife) saying, "Honey you'll never believe it, the clients said 'yes' and I'm going to make $300." It was only later that I appreciated the real cause for celebration had nothing to do with money. I was doing the right thing for the client. I had worked so hard to come up with the correct amount of insurance and the right type of policy. I had saved them money and provided protection for their family. I had performed as a professional, a concerned professional. The fact that I made any money was a happy bonus.

I realized that it takes considerable time and effort to do the right job well. It's a lesson I've tried to never forget. With an overload of clients, devoting the right time and effort to each account is physically impossible.

Is your advisor selective about adding clients or will he or she take anyone who has a pulse and a paycheck? Just as some advisors are a little difficult to deal with, some clients are too. Taking on difficult clients can be hazardous to a firm's health and also be a disservice to the other clients. There are a number of ways a good advisor should exercise caution in adding clients, and most would not be observable from the outside. One easy way to tell if your advisor is at all selective is finding out if they have an account minimum.

Brokers who are successful, service-oriented, and committed to their clients will always have an account minimum. They've analyzed how to balance their time with their clients' needs. They know how much time they'll spend with each client throughout the year and realize that to properly service their roster of clients and at the same time be profitable, only clients with certain account values can be accepted. Know your broker's account minimums and make sure your account is neither too big nor too small for that firm.

So what kind of account minimum should you look for? It depends on how much money you'll be entrusting to your advisor. If you'll be investing $100,000, you probably want to start with an advisor with a $100,000 minimum. If your account is larger you'll want to use a range of minimums depending on your advisor's services and expertise. Look at the table below to choose the advisor with the right account minimum for you:

Your account size	Advisor's account minimum
$100,000	$100,000
$500,000	$300,000 – $500,000
$1,000,000	$500,000 – $1,000,000
$3,000,000	$1,000,000 – $3,000,000
$5,000,000	$3,000,000 – $5,000,000
$10,000,000	$5,000,000+
$25,000,000	$10,000,000+
$50,000,000	$10,000,000+

While this table is not meant to suggest hard and fast rules, it offers good approximations. The greater level of assets you have, the more sophistication your advisor must have. He or she needs to have experience working with people of your wealth.

As a rule of thumb, don't go with someone where you'll be their smallest client or you may not get very good service. Also don't go with an advisor where you'll be their biggest client as they may not have the experience and/ or the tools to work with your situation.

Despite what I've just said, don't be afraid to work with someone who has a bit of flexibility. Here's what I mean. A few years ago, in the same week I met with one investor who had over $5,000,000 and another who had only $50,000. I realized that the $5,000,000 client was not a good fit for my firm at the time. That account would be no problem now, but back then we weren't equipped to properly manage a portfolio of that size. I declined the account.

The $50,000 account was below our minimum. But this client was a woman who had just lost her husband and really needed direction. Because I felt we could help her, she was someone we could not refuse. Most firms would not take $50,000 over $5,000,000 but that is what flexibility is all about. In the end it's only about serving the client.

(Saying that it's all about "serving the client" may sound corny, but over the long term this is a philosophy that pays big dividends. It's an investment in doing the right thing that sometimes may not yield profit short-term, but almost always creates growth in the future.)

Breaking it Down

There are genuinely different levels of sophistication needed to work with various levels of clients. If you're investing $300,000 or more, you should be working with someone who can work off of a fee basis (more on this later). Your portfolio should utilize either institutional mutual funds or exchange traded funds for their quality and low expense and you should **not** pay a commission for each transaction. You may not have anything elaborate or out of the ordinary in your portfolio but at this level, expenses become critical.

Once your portfolio reaches the $1,000,000–$3,000,000 mark, all of the above applies, but you also need to find an advisor who can add more alternative investments like non-publicly traded real estate (REITs), oil and gas offerings, and/or equipment leasing. These and other similar investments are not correlated to the overall stock market which can make them less volatile and can help stabilize your returns. These strategies all have net worth requirements for investment qualification. Too many brokers don't even know much about these types of products.

Institutional managers should be discussed and may be added to your portfolio. These managers allow you to set up your own personal mutual fund.

At the $5,000,000–$10,000,000 mark you're in the Ultra-High Net-Worth category. Your advisor should be presenting more options, such as a separate account manager who caters specifically to wealthy individuals and institutional investors. You're entitled to more of a personalized relationship with your manager. You'll likely hear about *structured investments* that allow you to choose from select offerings only available to investors of your stature. At this level, your investment advisor should have a good working relationship with both your accountant and attorney.

If you're at the $10,000,000–$100,000,000 level, an almost unlimited array of investments can be added to your investment selections. If you're working with an advisor who's used to dealing with $100,000 accounts, you're in trouble. Chances are very good that your advisor has no clue about the types of investment opportunities you should be focused on, opportunities such as going directly into a *private equity* offering or participating through a *feeder fund*. Utilizing structured products would also be offered, and it would be reasonable to have a structured product established specifically for you.

To understand the tools available in this category, *structured investments* utilize several investment types including futures, options, and leverage. These investments strive to achieve a multiple of a portfolio's upside while completely or partially protecting the portfolio from the downside. Because they are "structured" they can be designed in almost any way desirable for the investor.

Private equity firms are usually formed to buy public companies to take private or, more often, to buy private companies to take public. In either case the goal is to enhance the value of those companies for a substantial return. The principals of the private equity firm will usually retain a major share of the potential profit, but will not make any money until the investor's full investment has been returned. Often times, these firms offer a substantially larger potential return than most typical equity investments.

Most of the best known private equity firms have account minimums that are well beyond the reach of most investors, but there are other options such as *feeder funds*. Feeder funds are established by some companies to allow them to be the primary investor in a private equity investment. This creates the option of selling smaller shares to outside investors at substantially reduced minimums.

All of these investments have account minimums and/or qualifications for an investor to partake in the offering. Each could have a place in your portfolio allocation but remember, this is where having a true understanding of risk is essential and having a trusted advisor is beyond imperative.

Above $10,000,000 you should be dealing directly with a separate account manager, and you should be able to negotiate your pricing. Almost everything is negotiable as you go higher and higher up this investor chain. The one issue to keep in mind, this is the same game where Bernie Madoff played. Many of his clients thought they knew him and paid only passing attention to the details of their accounts. Only when it was too late did they figure out that he had falsified their returns.

Just make sure you're cautious and demanding in your expectations. The essence of your relationship with a financial advisor is you're paying that person to make good honest investment decisions. Make your advisor earn your trust.

Things Change

What if your investment portfolio grows toward the higher end of your advisor's portfolio range or your financial situation changes dramatically through an inheritance or buy-out for example? Then you may need to consider moving your assets to a firm better equipped to serve you.

I met with a husband and wife recently who had been using the same financial advisor for about 10 years. They were very appreciative of that advisor's work but now were in a different situation. The wife's mother had died and they received an inheritance of over $3 million.

Overnight their whole life turned around. Everything had just gotten a little easier...or had it? When they met with their financial advisor to see what to do with this newfound money, they were not impressed. He recommended continuing the same things they had already been doing. He did not focus on reducing risk, adding diversification, or even utilizing tax-efficient investing; although his recommendations did stand to make him substantial commissions.

The couple was not convinced that following his suggestions would put them in a better situation. After I met with them and saw what their planner had recommended, I realized they had outgrown his services. He lacked the knowledge, financial "sophistication" and experience to work effectively with their new account size. This mismatch had the potential to cost them a substantial amount of money.

It's critical that you choose a financial advisor who is qualified and suits your needs. It's just as critical that you find an advisor who's selective about working only with clients who are qualified, an advisor who's ready and able to serve your needs well.

The best financial advisors set account minimums. Your accounts need to fit comfortably within those minimums.

CHAPTER 6

Who's Making Money?

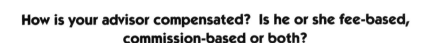

**How is your advisor compensated? Is he or she fee-based,
commission-based or both?**

Many investors don't understand how their broker makes money and that is a real problem. Some brokers work off of a commission while others charge a fee. Commissions are usually one-time payments for your broker and paid each time there is a transaction. These commissions can be paid out of your investment or hidden by higher expenses.

Fees are more transparent as they must be clearly stated and you must sign paperwork that clearly identifies the cost. Fees are most often annual and about 1% to 1.5% of the amount being managed.

Paying a fee is most appropriate beginning at the $300,000 to $400,000 portfolio value. The reason is this: let's say your planner is earning 1.5% on your account of $100,000, approximately $1,500 per year or $125 per month. At that level, the advisor is probably not making enough money to have sufficient incentive to give you any real level of attention. A fee three or four times that level begins to make sense for most advisors. The last thing you want is to work with an advisor who feels underpaid for the value he provides.

Let's examine fee versus commission a little more closely. When a broker is paid on commission it's not just for buying a security; it's for selling one too. So whether the market is going up or down doesn't matter, your broker is getting paid. Sometimes, brokers make **more** money when your accounts are going down than when they're going up.

When the market is going up, you may tell the broker to hold on to what you have so there are zero commissions and zero taxes. Conversely when the market moves down, the broker can justify making more trades trying to steer your investments in a positive direction. So you're paying more in commissions as your account potentially goes down.

In 1999 a woman who was referred to me, said her former stockbroker was making trades almost daily. Her trade confirmations filled a shoebox; there must have been 250 trade receipts for a single year. After doing some additional research, I found she'd made an okay rate of return, but it was below the overall market return at the time. There were more realized gains and thus more taxes to be paid and the broker made more in commissions than she made in her portfolio. In the end, she took him in front of an arbitration panel and won almost all of her commission cost back. But, she still didn't get close to market returns and still had a higher tax bill.

This woman was the victim of the greatest danger with a commission-based account: *churning*. If your broker is getting paid on each transaction, there is the risk that an unethical advisor will make an inordinate number of trades, more in an effort to generate commissions than profit for you, the investor. Churning is a violation of securities law and can lead to a fine or suspension of the advisor.

Many financial planners who get paid commissions are trying to get you a good solid return and that, after all, is supposed to be their mission. But sometimes it's hard to tell the difference between a conscientious advisor and one who's making an unjustifiable number of trades. My advice is to be cautious and always look at your transaction expenses relative to your returns.

With a fee-based arrangement there is no risk of churning. The fee is generally paid on a quarterly basis. So if the fee is 1% then the brokerage company would take a snapshot view of the account on the last day of each quarter and 25 basis points (.25%) of that account value would be deducted from the cash portion of your account. As the account balance goes up the fee would be higher, and as the account goes down the fee (and your advisor's paycheck) would be lower. With this arrangement your broker has incentive to make your account go up. This arrangement puts both the advisor and the client on the same side of the table.

Often there are very few, if any, account expenses beyond your fee and absolutely no commissions paid with this arrangement. In this scenario, the broker isn't worried about trying to sell you something, instead there's motivation to find better opportunities to put in your portfolio to help that portfolio go up in value.

The "Mother Rule"

Clients are always at risk in the relationship they have with their financial planners. Clients are the ones with the accounts that can go down. They are the ones who pay for our services with their cold hard cash, and ultimately, they are the ones taking all of the risk.

The advisor has very little actual risk. If the market goes down, it's not the advisor's money that goes down. If the advisor loses a client there are plenty more that will help pay the rent. If the advisor chooses the wrong course of action he or she only loses a little income.

The client, however, could lose everything and a good advisor always remembers that.

An advisor needs to always think from the client's perspective. He needs to be so in tune with his clients that if the market goes down he feels like he's lost his own money. Before he recommends something, he needs to thoroughly investigate it from all angles. If he uses *The Mother Rule* he's spot on. He should constantly ask himself, "Would this investment be one I would recommend to my own mother?" And if it is, then it should be a good investment for his client.

If you know that your advisor follows The Mother Rule, it should give you a solid measure of confidence. (Assuming he and Mom have a good relationship.)

An Investment Advisor

The other thing to remember about a fee-based system is that in order for your advisor to charge a fee, he or she must pass a certification exam to become a Registered Investment Advisor (RIA). Taking exams may seem perfunctory but it can be an important indicator of your advisor's competence.

A number of years ago I was working at an insurance brokerage firm where several of the planners were taking the Series 65 Investment Advisory exam. Passing the exam would give them the right to charge fees for asset management and financial planning. One of the test takers was not a particularly good planner based on his financial knowledge and experience. He actually took the exam four times without passing. After each failure, he had a waiting period before he could attempt the test again. But over and over he failed.

At the time I felt sorry for him, but now that I look back I understand that the system worked. It kept him from being able to hold a license that was beyond his capabilities. Quite honestly I believe that had he gotten that license it would have been to the detriment of his clients.

Most designations in the industry do not come easily and are an indication that your advisor has a solid foundation of knowledge.

The Registered Investment Advisor license has several implications, the most important of which requires a higher level of responsibility in the advisor-client relationship. The automatic ongoing fiduciary responsibility inherent in charging a fee means there is a legal obligation for the RIA to do the "right thing" for each client to the best of his ability. You would think such a requirement would be extended to every advisory relationship but only in a fee-based relationship is the advisor legally bound to operate diligently.

When charging you a fee, your advisor has a requirement to deliver a document to you called the ADV Part II. This is simply the authorization that shows that they are allowed to charge a fee and how much it can be. The ADV is an interesting read for insomniacs, right up there with a prospectus.

I often hear this question about fee-based advisors, "If my account goes down, why should my advisor get paid at all?" The theory is that the advisor didn't do a good job so there should be no fee. The simple answer is that the FINRA rules say the broker cannot participate directly in your gains or losses. Compensation can only be based on that stated fee no matter which way the market is going.

Think of it another way, if you work for a company and the profits for the company go down, should you still get paid? Of course you should, because you're still working in the best interest of that business. That's the same way it is with your fee-based advisor.

It's my belief that your accounts should do better than the market for an advisor to earn his keep. This is true in both up and down markets. I don't necessarily mean that you'll always make money. I mean that if the market goes down 10%, your account may go down but by a factor of less than 10%. Again, I suggest you look at this return over complete market cycles (meaning several years), not over months or on a day to day basis.

As an example, think of the market we had in 2008. We all know how bad that year of the market cycle was. But just in case you don't remember, the S&P 500 was down a thoroughly depressing 37%. Yes, I said 37%. Of course if you waited until March 9 of 2009 the market lost an additional 25% in just nine weeks (when the S&P 500 closed at 676.53).

At that point many people were looking at their advisor saying, "What the heck are you doing? You just lost more than half of my portfolio over twelve and a half months!" And you would be right in saying that. Many people fired their advisors **that** week. A good number even sold everything and put their money in cash. But that is not the end of the story.

Over the next few weeks, as of May 18, 2009 when the S&P 500 closed at 909.03, the market had recovered 34% in about 70 days. If you were invested in cash, you didn't receive any of that rebound. I'm not saying that your advisor should follow the index; you could do that yourself. But I am saying that relying on a good advisor to help you through the worst of markets can make him worth his weight in gold. (Of course, many people would have swapped their advisor for some gold, but that option wasn't available.)

Variations on Commissions

We've discussed the most straightforward way that advisors receive a commission, but what other ways do brokers get paid commissions?

Mutual funds create a variety of possibilities. If the mutual fund is a commissioned fund, it is an A, B, or C share. "A" shares typically charge an upfront commission that is usually about 4–6% of the amount invested. Most often at least half of that amount goes to the broker, the rest goes to the broker's firm (broker/dealer). So think of it this way, if you invest $10,000 and the commission is 5% then only $9,500 of your dollars are invested and $500 is split between the broker and his firm.

If your broker recommends a "B" share fund (commonly known as a *back-end load* fund), you will not be charged an upfront fee, but the broker still gets paid by the fund company. In this case, if you invest $10,000 your full $10,000 goes to work for you in the market. The big difference is that you have now committed those assets to the fund company for approximately six or seven years. If you take your money out of the fund before that time has elapsed you could be charged a *surrender penalty*, somewhat like a bank charges a penalty for early withdrawal of a CD.

Usually there is a surrender schedule that the fund will follow with a prescribed penalty corresponding to the year you take the money out. As an example, the schedule might be something like 6% in year one then 5,5,4,3, and 2% in the following years; which means if you take out your money in the first year, you will be charged a 6% penalty. In the fifth year your withdrawal would cost a penalty of 3%. The penalty can be charged on the initial investment or on the current value, it depends on the fund company. All these details are explained in that wonderful sleep-provoking prospectus.

The problem with the B share fund is the expense ratio (the cost charged internally by each mutual fund to cover legal, accounting, management, and overhead expenses). This ratio is usually much higher than it would be for an A share, and you have to leave your money with that B fund company for years and years before the surrender penalty is lifted and before the high internal expense of the fund is lowered.

So that leaves the "C" share mutual fund. This fund is known as a *level-load fund*. When you purchase a C share, you're not hit with any upfront cost or any back-end surrender penalties, but you are charged an internal expense cost for as long as you hold the fund. There is usually a 1% surrender charge if you pull your money out in the first year but withdrawals after year one do not carry a charge. The C share does, however, charge you a higher internal expense similar to the B share. It's usually 1% higher than A shares and this 1% is split between the broker and his firm.

On the other side of the commission-based mutual fund equation is the *no-load* (no commission) *fund*. These funds are sometimes called the "no advice" funds because when you purchase a fund, there is no broker and the company from which you purchase cannot give you any advice on which particular investments to buy. A lot of do-it-yourselfers use this kind of fund and do their own research. No-load funds have no upfront charges, no back-end surrender charges and no level-loads either. So they are usually much less expensive than their commission-based counterparts but you are left on your own to decide what to buy.

There are also *institutional funds* which are often the best of all worlds. They do not charge a commission and have some of the lowest expense ratios. These funds are generally for the fund company's largest clients (with accounts of $1,000,000 – $5,000,000). Most often you'll find these funds are used in a fee-based account.

The chart below illustrates the difference between an A share, B share, C share, no-load, and institutional share funds. It shows the upfront cost, the back-end surrender charge, and the expense ratio and gives a good idea of how much these funds actually charge.

	Front Load	Backend Load	Annual Expense Ratio
A share	5.75%	0%	.45%
B share	0%	6,5,5,4,3,2%	1.75%
C share	0%	1% yr one only	1.75%
No-Load	0%	0%	.45%
Institutional	0%	0%	.35%

To better understand the expenses with mutual funds suppose you invested $100,000 in each type of fund. $100,000 in an A Share would cost $5,750 up front (disregarding discounts for the large amount invested) and the internal expense charged annually would be .45% ($450) of the account balance for as long as you own the fund. $100,000 in a 'B' share would be fully invested with no upfront cost but an annual expense of 1.75% ($1,750/yr) for about 6–7 years until the shares change to "A". At that point the annual internal expense charge would change to .45%. $100,000 in a C share would be fully invested with no upfront charge and an annual expense of 1.75% ($1,750/yr) **and** you must stay in the fund for at least one year to avoid a 1% penalty. The 1.75% would be charged for the life of your account. $100,000 in a no-load would be fully invested with no upfront cost but an annual internal expense charge of .45% ($450) of the account balance for as long as you own the fund. $100,000 in an institutional fund would be fully invested with no upfront cost but an annual internal expense charge of .35% ($350) of the account balance for as long as you own the fund. While the no-load and institutional funds look like the best scenario overall, they may not always be the best choice. In many fee-based investment accounts, A share funds can usually be purchased without a load. These funds are commonly known as *load-waived*. It is important to appreciate this fact when choosing funds for a fee-based, asset management account as the load-waived A shares can have the best and most consistent performance.

It's not uncommon to see mutual funds handled ineptly in someone's portfolio. A local couple came into my office last January. They had made a New Year's resolution to get another opinion on their investments.

When I looked at their portfolio, I saw something that could get their advisor in a lot of trouble. They had many, many different mutual funds. These funds were all commissionable, but that's not the real issue. The problem was that over four years the advisor had put some of their money in A share funds, some in B share funds, and even some in C share funds.

On some of the mutual funds the advisor received upfront commissions, and on others, he received a quarterly check to pay for service he was not providing. He clearly wasn't monitoring the account and also never called the clients. And to top it off, because of the large amount of money this couple had invested and because it was all long-term, their money should have been put entirely into A shares. In this class of funds, they would have received a significant break on the upfront commission and the ongoing expenses would have been about **seventy percent** lower.

An even more economical strategy would have been to utilize a fee-based account with an annual fee that would have cost them significantly less and given their advisor more fiduciary responsibility.

They'd been victimized by an advisor who either didn't understand mutual funds or was simply unethical.

So where does that leave us? Here are some rules of thumb: A shares are better for larger investments and for the long term. B shares work well with smaller investments and for intermediate timeframes. C shares are used when you plan to add funds to an investment periodically and/or plan to hold the investment for a shorter period of time. No-loads are for do-it-yourselfers who want to do their own research and choose their own portfolio. Finally, institutional funds are usually found in fee-based accounts, not available to everyone, but often can offer the best value and performance. A good advisor will know what's right for your situation.

CHAPTER 7

Your Risk...and Reward

Is your advisor sufficiently risk and tax conscious?

I met with a gentleman in 2001 who came to my office after being in the audience at one of my workshops. He wanted a second opinion about his portfolio. I had asked him to bring copies of his tax returns, wills and trust documents, and all of his investment statements.

As we began to go over his records, I first looked at his wills and trusts and everything seemed to be in order. His tax returns showed he wasn't paying an exorbitant amount in taxes.

Finally I looked at his investment statements. He handed me a large stack of envelopes secured by a rubber band. As I began pulling envelopes out, I noticed that **none** of them had been opened. I said, "Sir, how do you know how your accounts are doing if you haven't opened any of the statements?" He had a funny but scary response, "After the market started to go down, I couldn't bear to watch it anymore so I stopped opening the envelopes." I did my best to hide my dismay.

As crazy as this example sounds, it's more common than you would imagine. What's far worse, many advisors have only a cursory knowledge of exactly where their clients stand on a regular basis. And they have even less of an appreciation for where their clients could end up.

What are the chances of the market going up? How about the chances of it going down? What's the chance of your portfolio going up or down? It's confounding how few brokers and/or investors ever really think about probabilities.

I know you studied very hard in your college statistics class, pulled off an "A" and never really thought about it again. You're not alone. Most people worry about risk in an abstract way without appreciating how risky their portfolio may be. More importantly, they never attempt to quantify that risk.

You Can Measure Risk

You MUST know the level of risk in any investment you make. Many investors have no idea what level of risk they're taking in their employer retirement plan, in their IRA, or even in their kids' college fund. Why not? Too few people understand how to measure it.

I want you to come away from this book appreciating the level of risk you take in the market every day. Just knowing that can help you make decisions whether the market is stable or volatile.

Warren Buffet recently said, "Be fearful when others are greedy and be greedy when others are fearful." What he's actually saying is to do the opposite of what everyone else is doing.

There's another old saying, "The definition of insanity is doing the same thing over and over and expecting different results." I'll take that a step further and say that if you do what everyone does, you will get what everyone else gets. And that, my friend, is the definition of mediocrity.

So you need to be different when investing by using a financial planner who knows how much risk you're taking in every investment. And beyond that, your advisor needs to know how the risk changes as you combine assets in a portfolio. For example, the more asset classes you have, the lower your risk level (not assets like different stocks, but asset classes like international stocks versus domestic stocks). If you add enough asset classes, you can take your risk level down so low that it can be half the general market risk. And you can still outperform the market, especially over the long run.

So how do you quantify risk? We have to bring back one of your favorite formulas from statistics class, the *standard deviation*. In simplest terms the formula is represented by the old bell curve: the more variable a set of data, the wider the bell shape; the less variable, the thinner the shape.

To understand risk you should also understand *volatility*, which is the potential for an investment to go up or down. But the question still remains, to be up and down from where? Most investments will have an expected return based on their history. Let's say with stocks, it's 10%. So the question is, how much does that investment fluctuate around the 10% mark?

You could have an investment that has averaged a return of 10% per year for the last 5 years, but at one point it was up 50% and at several other points it was down more than 25%. In this case, it may not be worth the anxiety and loss of sleep to get that 10% return. Or maybe it is. The point is you can know, going in, whether to expect such variation.

If we equate that variability (volatility) to all your investments, the more unpredictability in your investment returns (meaning they're all over the board versus very close to an average) the higher the *standard deviation* and vice versa. Standard deviation is expressed as a number, the lower the number the lower the risk. A stock portfolio will have a much higher standard deviation than a bond portfolio.

For those who like math, think of it this way. If we have an investment that has an average return of 10% with a standard deviation of 5, then there is a 68.2% chance of the investment returning within 1 standard deviation (5%) higher or lower than the average (in this case it could be 5% to 15%). A standard deviation of 8 is riskier and 10 even more risky. Greek, right?

It may seem a little complicated but at the end of the day, understanding the real risk of your portfolio is a very important step in determining how high your portfolio could rise but also how low it could fall.

If you know the average return and the standard deviation of an investment, then you have a really good idea how it will perform. But again, most brokers don't understand risk themselves and are consequently unable to explain it to their clients. "It's just too complicated," they'd say.

I beg to differ. Risk can be explained! It's one of the single most important aspects of your portfolio.

Not long ago my firm was one of three financial planning companies invited to give a presentation to a private foundation. They had a significant endowment fund that was not invested well and were considering hiring a new group to handle the portfolio. We were asked to give a presentation to their Investment Committee for forty-five minutes and then take questions for another fifteen minutes.

When it was our time to present, I had broken down our presentation into three segments. The first segment included a slide of the standard deviation of their current portfolio. In the simplest terms, I talked about this concept as it related to their level of risk. I then talked about the upside and downside of their current portfolio and then compared it to our suggested investment mix. In fifteen minutes they realized their current investment strategy was far too risky.

Next, I talked about their current investment policy constraints. They had a document that set rules about what types of investments they could and could not use in their portfolio. The major problem with these rules was that they were written nearly 20 years ago when the investing world was completely different. I helped them understand what changes they should make to their investment policies and how these changes would be helpful to them and their new investment firm, no matter who it was.

Finally, I spent a short time on the specific investment portfolio I recommended for their endowment. I didn't have to spend much time on it because I had just explained in the first thirty minutes exactly how I came up with these recommendations. So they already completely understood my approach.

At the end of the Q&A, all of the investment committee members sincerely thanked me for making things so easy to understand. Several even asked me to review their own portfolios. We ended up working with that foundation as well as with many of the members on that original investment committee.

The reason we were successful is because we educated the members in a clear and simple way and helped them understand the critical role "risk" plays in determining the most appropriate investments.

Wouldn't it be nice to know what to expect in the worst case as well as in the best-case scenarios? For most kinds of investments the information is available to make these risk calculations with great accuracy. Your broker must have a working knowledge of risk, plus the ability and willingness to explain it to you.

Most brokers can describe in general terms a "conservative" investor at one end of the spectrum, a "growth" investor at the other end, and the "growth and income" investor who is right in the middle. As a client, you can answer a set of questions for them and they'll lump you into one of those broad categories.

What does that information actually tell your advisor or you? Is there anything quantifiable about that "data"? The answer is NO! It's a conveniently vague generality that doesn't scratch the surface of the science of investing.

The common belief is that investing is an elusive art. Successful advisors may pore over batches of numbers, but in the end it's really back to dart throwing. This is the way many advisors approach investing, but the real truth is that understanding the numbers and volatility and standard deviation allows the savvy advisor to actually control the range of risk in a portfolio to a significant degree.

The market may go down 25% in a month, and many advisors will see their clients' accounts go down by a similar percentage. They'll shrug and say, "Well, no one can control the market."

It is very possible to design a portfolio that's resistant to this kind of major drop. When the market went down 38% in the fall of 2008, I had a category of portfolios that ranged from a gain of 24% to a drop of 27%, depending on each client's desired the level of risk. These portfolios were specifically designed to withstand major drops in the market.

Now that I've piqued your interest, I'll elaborate on the importance of standard deviation. Standard deviation (SD) is a formula to measure risk. It's based on what we call a *normal distribution* which is just a set of data (rates of return in this case) that usually are all distributed around an average. That means some returns are higher and some are lower than the average, but the measurable data points are still fairly close to the average.

What the SD is telling you is how closely all of the data points come to that average. The more closely the data points are set to each other, the lower the standard deviation, the more distant the points, the higher the standard deviation. For example, in 2008 the SD of the S&P 500 was 20, while the SD of a 90-day Treasury bill (T-bill) was 1. Clearly the T-bill was a safer, less volatile investment.

From a risk/return standpoint, you want a higher average return with a lower standard deviation.

Here's a simple example of standard deviation. I can predict the high temperature in Washington D.C. on any day of the week four months or even four years from now. I do that by looking at the historical highs for that day for as long as meteorologists have measured and recorded such data. I can look at the entire range of temperatures for that day and know the average temperature and the "volatility" of extremes above and below the average. And I can know the statistical likelihood of that high temperature varying from the average temperature. Using this information, I can predict the high temperature and know the probability of the temperature differing from my prediction.

By studying the historical volatility of an investment, the SD predicts the statistical range of future volatility.

What is critical to understand about risk is that it's not an abstract generalization but a definable number, as measurable and predictable as the temperature on a given day. The person handling your investments must have a total understanding of risk because it's the main tool for having a measure of control in an investment world that sometimes looks out of control.

Keeping What You've Earned

And that brings us to *tax efficiency*.

Certainly it's an understatement to say that income taxes are important. We all have to pay them and all understand their critical role in the U.S. economy and government. But who wants to pay more than they're legally obligated to pay? You can minimize your taxes, but you must work with people who know the rules.

The best financial advisors will be very well informed about the tax code and the never-ending changes impacting it. Your advisor should work with your accountant to keep him or her informed of your investment gains and losses. Most advisors know to strategically sell losing investments at the end of the year to limit your tax exposure. A good advisor will also search for ways to defer taxes whenever possible and appropriate, especially for long-term investments.

Here's an example: assume you have $100,000 that's growing at 10% per year for 10 years. You can structure the tax on that investment in several ways, but here are two of the most straightforward. Investment A is taxed at a 50% tax each year (we'll assume a 50% tax rate to make it easier to understand). Investment B is tax-deferred so that the tax is paid when the money is withdrawn.

Investment A	**Investment B**
Taxable @ 50%	*Tax Deferred/ultimately taxed at 50%*

Value at the end of ten years:

$162,889	$259,374

Average annual income in year 11+ (**after tax**):

$ 8,144	$ 12,969

By deferring the tax, the principal grows much more quickly. You are, in effect, compounding the interest. In short, you end up with considerably more money after 10 years if you defer the tax, and your income could be almost 50% higher. This is just one approach that your investment advisor can help you with.

Your advisor needs to think about tax efficiency throughout the year because it can really effect your ultimate account value. The key is that your advisor must understand the tax code and work with your accountant. Otherwise you lose.

I had a new client who, previous to our relationship, had put a considerable amount of money into an account on which he was going to pay tax each year. When I asked him what the money was for, he said he probably wouldn't need it and would likely just transfer it to his kids after he was gone. So I asked, "Why are you paying tax on money you'll never use? If it's for your kids, let your kids pay the tax; they'll ultimately end up with more money anyway."

He agreed. We changed the investment into a tax-deferred portfolio. That simple move saved him (and his children) a lot of money.

Always, always remember, it's not how much you make, it's how much you KEEP!

CHAPTER 8
Long Term Thinker

Does your advisor run an independent and proper business? Does he or she operate as a real business? How can you tell if your advisor is serious about the profession?

F reedom, in my mind, is essential for good financial planning. Many advisors are not free to make their own independent decisions about your account. If they work for one of the big Internet-based houses or mega brokerage firms, chances are they will be pushed to sell certain products and to make recommendations based on what the company wants.

An **independent** advisor, on the other hand, will be free to find the best strategies for your particular situation. Independence allows your advisor to do research and come up with the best possible recommendations that fit your personal risk parameters and ultimate investing goals.

In this world of big investment companies (even though there are fewer now and the government owns a piece of some of the remaining ones) clients are often treated as a number rather than as a person. I've frequently seen an investor get shuffled around to one broker after another because their previous advisor got a promotion or moved on.

I've also spoken to many individuals who signed on with a company, were given an 800 number to call, and subsequently were never able to speak to the same person consistently. This is assembly line investing. No one at the firm knows them or their families or anything about them other than what their personal profile screen reveals. This parade of advisors doesn't have the time to find out who their customers really are. With independence comes personal service. Your advisor needs to know who you are before they can best determine how to serve you.

Over the last ten years, I've met with a number of people who worked with a certain large financial planning company. When I met with these people and found out what company handled their investments, I could *always* predict almost exactly what was in their portfolio. Advisors from this particular company used the same investments with all of their clients. While this may sound okay if it's a good portfolio, the problem is that there were never any changes to their mix of investments. I mean never. This strategy assumed that every client had the same risk tolerance and objectives, which is absurd.

This particular company used the same investments over and over, even when the investments were no longer the best in class. I've seen this approach with this company for the last 10 years. Every one of their clients had identical investments because their advisor was doing nothing but following the corporate recommendations and selling the company's product. This is an advisor not just falling asleep at the helm but falling off the boat completely.

Independence is a choice your advisor makes when he or she gets into the financial service profession. Running a business, however, is not a choice it's a given. Your advisor is running a business to make money, and you should hope he or she does. Those who don't make money are out of business. Financial advisors are often like other skilled people such as artists or chefs; they're frequently great at their craft but not good at the business of keeping the doors open. They may be capable of developing great portfolios but can't manage people, structure, or even cash flow.

Why is this important? Let me give you an example. A few years ago, my wife and I hired a masonry company to build pillars at the end of the driveway to our house. You could tell by the owner's drawings that he really had a gift for masonry. He was clearly skilled and we were confident his work was going to look great. So we hired him, signed a contract, and gave him a fifty percent deposit.

Within a few days he and his crew were working diligently. Everything was going well until the end of the first week. The owner/artist of the company came to me and said he needed more money. He apologetically told me that he'd miscalculated the amount of material required and needed to raise his cost estimate. Being a trusting soul, I obliged.

During the four-week job he came to me two more times for unscheduled payments. I felt badly that he couldn't pay his workers so I gave him the additional amounts. Finally, I put my foot down when he tried to charge me additional at the end of the job because of his ongoing miscalculations. Fortunately by then the job was completed and I didn't have to deal with him again.

The guy was a great person but a terrible businessman and I suffered because of it. This was just bricks and concrete, but what happens when your financial advisor is a poor businessperson and your financial future is at stake?

When your advisor is not a good businessperson, you may not be getting the attention you deserve. The advisor is probably wasting large amounts of time herding the cats in his office at the expense of your account. Time that should be spent studying the markets in relation to your account is spent putting out fires in the office and figuring out how to pay the electric bill.

How do you know if your advisor is a capable business professional?

Focus on the details of his business. A sizable staff may be a good sign of your advisor's commitment. If you're working with a one-person operation, plain and simple, you have a recipe for disaster. Your representative is doing too many jobs: marketing to new clients, meeting with current clients, managing investments, handling paperwork, fielding emails and phone calls, paying the bills, and trying to live a life outside of work.

A financial planning business cannot be run by one person or even two for that matter. Make sure your advisor has at least two assistants and preferably more. To service clients takes time, to manage investments well takes even more time. To run an office requires a trained, efficient staff. A true professional will have one or more people helping with each of these jobs.

This staffing will insure that you will not have to be searching for a new planner in a couple of years when your current one gets overwhelmed and stops doing a good job with your portfolio.

A Long Term Business

An advisor must run a successful business in order to be in business in the future. Unless your advisor has a plan for the future, you soon may be without an advisor because his business will have failed. That doesn't necessarily mean that your broker actually goes out of business. As a matter of fact, going out of business would be preferable to what often happens: the advisor flounders for a significant period of time trying hard to save the business. During that time no one is managing your account or having review meetings with you. Eventually you get irate and find a new broker.

An advisor committed to his business must focus on longevity and service. With such a commitment the advisor is taking what he earns from the practice and putting some of it back to work in his company. He is continuously investing in his business, hiring more support staff, finding conveniently located office space, reviewing investment and financial planning tools (software), hiring expert speakers for client events, and spending money on professional development. All of these investments lead to an enhancement in two areas: better financial planning and better service. Those are the areas where the advisor should excel and areas that will impact you the most.

It's sometimes difficult to tell if your advisor has spent his income on a new beach house instead of tools to enhance the business but more often, it's obvious. Look at the office; is it clean, well decorated, and organized? Is there always someone to greet you? If paperwork needs to be done, does your advisor do it or is there a designated person who does all paperwork for the office? When you call with a service-related question, do you have to wait for a call back or is there a designated person who handles all phone calls?

One thing to always keep in mind is that, across the board, the reason most businesses fail is lack of capital and lack of knowledge. The nice thing about capital investment is that it's easy to see. When the business owner hasn't put enough money back into things like infrastructure the problems are usually obvious. This infrastructure is the very thing that will make the business successful, viable and a good experience for you. Knowledge is more difficult to measure.

A Measure of Commitment

The easiest way to get a sense of your advisor's business acumen is to look at his business card. Is it a blank card with just a name and contact information or does it show a profusion of recognitions after the name? Obtaining professional designations is not only costly but it takes a tremendous time commitment, follow through, and intelligence.

You want your advisor to have any of the following designations (the more the better):

CFP	Certified Financial Planner
ChFC	Chartered Financial Consultant
RIA	Registered Investment Advisor
CHMC	Chartered Mutual Fund Counselor
CIMA	Certified Investment Management Analyst
CFA	Chartered Financial Analyst
CPA	Certified Public Accountant
JD	Juris Doctor
EA	Enrolled Agent

Believe me, these designations are not easy to obtain. Most require having significant industry experience, taking educational courses, passing a cumulative certification exam, plus completing ongoing continuing education requirements. If your planner has attained any of these designations, he's done a lot of work and has shown a commitment to the financial industry.

The best financial advisor always strives to be both astute and current in the field and has professional designations to prove it.

Having a Long Term View

The best financial advisor will always have a business succession plan. At the next meeting with your broker, ask what happens to your account if something happens to him or her. Many brokers build succession plans for their clients but don't have one for their own business. What happens if they leave the firm, get fired, get sick or even die? Are you left out in the cold?

Having an organized plan is the sign of a committed financial professional. It also shows a genuine concern for your success, irrespective of the advisor's status.

If your advisor has indeed put together a plan, that plan should be explainable without hesitation. Some of the best financial planning offices even have a succession plan document to give you even more comfort about their vision for the future. You need to be assured your investments will be monitored no matter what happens to your advisor.

(For other key questions to ask your advisor, go to www.fireyourbroker.com.)

CHAPTER 9

Bernie's Buddy

Does your advisor have a clean record?

Now we're back to Bernie Madoff. Here's a guy who bilked millions of dollars from so-called friends, charities, even family members, not to mention hundreds of unsuspecting investors attracted by big returns and famous clients.

How can you trust anyone after you hear such a frightening story? Madoff was able to invent phantom returns right under the eyes of the Securities and Exchange Commission.

If an unscrupulous advisor can fool the SEC, how can you keep it from happening to you? How do you make sure that your advisor isn't a disciple of the Madoff school of corruption?

Ironically, part of the issue was that Madoff's investors were of such wealth that the SEC figured they could police their own investments. Smaller investors actually have more protection from regulatory agencies than the big dogs.

Still, how can you tell that your investments are at risk when the very statements you use to review them have been falsified? Thankfully the regulations put upon securities truly provide protection for the average investor.

Most securities must be registered products. They would be registered with FINRA (Financial Industry Regulatory Authority) or with the SEC (Securities and Exchange Commission). Because they are registered, the securities must follow a significant set of guidelines.

Most of Madoff's holdings were not registered and so there was very little oversight.

One way for an investor to stay safe is to make sure your advisor only uses registered products. How do you know what those products are? Registered investments will include such things as: stocks, bonds, mutual funds, Exchange Traded Funds, Unit Investment Trusts, and Variable Annuities.

Many non-registered investments are considered *private placements* which means they are investments made directly with a company, entity, or person. Because of this direct type of investment, they do not require the registration and / or regulation of most securities. This inherently can make them more risky.

Registered investments are usually sold by a *prospectus*, another document almost guaranteed to put you to sleep. But the prospectus features facts about the company and the offering and an elaboration on the risks involved.

Out of all of the clients we've ever had, I would guess that maybe 5% have ever read a prospectus cover to cover. Further, I would say the number of advisors who have fully read a prospectus cover-to-cover is maybe slightly higher than 10%. They are not an interesting read. But I will say that the more of them you read the easier it becomes to zero in on the important parts. That's a skill worth developing.

Another thing you can do to verify your investment portfolio mix is to call the company that actually holds the account. Your advisor will usually hold all client accounts within his or her brokerage firm. This firm will *custody* your portfolio, which means they offer an account to hold and report on your securities, allow trades to be executed, and print monthly statements. So essentially the firm is a third party which can be verified. For example, if your broker is affiliated with Morgan Stanley, you can call Morgan Stanley directly to verify any positions in your account.

When you call the brokerage firm you can verify your holdings by asking amounts, prices, and recent transactions. Do this periodically as your own personal audit. Making this check a couple of times per year insures that your statements are not being falsified. Just be certain that there is an arm's length agreement between your advisor and the brokerage firm. Madoff was his own firm, so there was no independent way to verify trades.

Find Verification on the Internet

Another thing you can do to confirm your financial advisor's reputation is check with the Financial Industry Regulatory Authority and the Securities and Exchange websites (www.FINRA.org and www.SEC.gov). All brokers and/or advisors have a registration number. By finding out that number (just ask) or by simply visiting these websites and inputting your advisor's name, you can get some great information. Each of these websites has a "broker check" section. You can see if there's been any regulatory action taken against your financial advisor. You can also see where that person is licensed, which licenses he or she holds, and when those licenses were received. On the SEC website, you can find out the total investments the advisor manages and how long he has been managing money under a fee-based arrangement.

Finally, if your broker has any professional designations you can obtain a status report from the regulatory authority that oversees each of those designations. On my website, www.fireyourbroker.com, you'll see all of the various web addresses which allow you to review your advisor's credentials.

Most often, when you click to any of these sites and find your broker's name, the information will be a little different than you might expect. On these websites when there is information listed, then there may be a problem. That likely means there was some type of issue or regulatory action against your advisor. So usually when you check these sites, no news is good news.

As a final level of comfort, I recommend a network that certifies advisors, called the Paladin Registry (www.paladinregistry.com). While I do pay a monthly fee to be part of it, they conduct their own research into my history and make me jump through many hoops to achieve the five-star rating I enjoy. Any advisor who is well-reviewed by this organization is doing everything in his power to demonstrate the ethics of his operation.

Can you still get duped by a Madoff type? Perhaps, but if you employ the due diligence mentioned above, you will all but eliminate the risk of this happening. The point is, make your advisor earn your trust and do not be shy about asking for documentation and confirmation of anything related to your account.

Most advisors are scrupulously honest. Your diligence insures you're enjoying the services of one of the good guys.

CHAPTER 10

Dirty Little Secrets

What is your advisor doing behind your back that benefits him at your expense?

It's fair to say that most individuals, families, groups, and even companies have secrets, skeletons in the closet, things they don't want everyone to know about. Most of the time these secrets only pertain to things that are potentially embarrassing. In the investment world there are, unfortunately, secret practices that go well beyond being embarrassing.

Would it surprise you to learn that your advisor may have some secrets that can adversely affect your account but benefit him?

"Why," you ask, "would a company allow things to happen that aren't in the best interest of the investor?" Good question. Some of these things are anomalies and really don't happen that often. Others are commonplace and just plain WRONG!

Some of these questionable practices are old bad habits that are hard to break and are still being done while others have been regulated, but not eradicated. Some, in my opinion, are just thinly disguised theft. Greed is a powerful motivator. It all starts with brokers trying to make more money on a trade, a recommendation, or even a sales pitch. In the end, the broker potentially makes a few more dollars, but the investors lose money or their returns are not what they should be.

Many brokers will applaud me for bringing these practices to light but, after this book, I may not be on the holiday card list for some others.

My introduction to questionable practices took place at one of my first jobs with a large investment firm nearly twenty years ago. At this firm I was given a lineup of mutual fund families to present to my clients. I naturally assumed that the company had done a lot of due diligence on these funds to insure each was the best possible offering. In the end what I found out really startled me.

First of all, what I realized (after doing some research) was that some of these mutual fund companies did not have many (or any) top-rated funds within their group. So I asked my superiors why we would use such a fund group. The answer I heard was completely unexpected and a little scary. I was told that those mutual fund companies had invested a lot of money in our company and that the "education trip" I had just taken was paid for by that mutual fund's corporate office. In essence, they paid their way onto our list of "preferred" investments.

It was clear to me that the companies with the biggest purse strings were the ones I was supposed to offer to my clients. In addition to striking me as unethical, I could see that this was a recipe for mediocrity. Many of the funds were not at the top of their game. Heck, when I compared their statistics to other similar funds they weren't even on the field.

So I told my company that I did not want to use those funds. They immediately told me that I could not use funds other than those they recommended. In other words, I could not use funds that would put my client in a better position. I could not recommend a higher quality fund that was more beneficial to my client's portfolio.

It was ludicrous. I have always felt investors deserve the best possible investments that I can get for them. Clients do not deserve investments that pay their way into favor. Suddenly, I was embarrassed for my industry. Even though I was a pawn in the system, I knew then that I would not be bound by such a ridiculous, unfair, unethical program. In my company today, we have no such rules. The client's needs are always paramount, always!

Another issue that bothered me while working for that same employer was how the company trained us to put together portfolios. Again we could offer only a select group of fund families, a small percentage of which were top-rated funds. Our client's money went into those funds with little regard for asset allocation. When I look back at those portfolios, most were not diversified into the different asset classes I talk about earlier in this book. At best, they were merely put into funds that did well last year.

As I interview potential new clients and look at their portfolios, it's obvious to me that the same kind of restrictions still exist in some of the major investment companies. People come into my office after one of my workshops and their current portfolios remind me of the old days. Simply put, these unsuspecting investors are taking too much risk, they are not diversified, and their portfolios are full of mediocre investments.

You'll recall that I talked earlier about the importance of your advisor being free to choose the best investments for each client's needs and goals. When an overbearing company restricts the advisor's choices it's almost always the client who suffers.

It can get worse. In a *wire house,* where investment bankers actually "manufacture" investments (meaning that they underwrite stock and bond holdings for companies), some shenanigans border on illegal. Questionable "opportunities" arise when they take a company public or when they assist a firm with a bond offering to the general public.

In my office there is an investment specialist who has extensive experience working for the two of the large U.S. wire house companies. He's one of my sources for information about the "secrets" of some investment firms.

Wire house companies underwrite different kinds of investments depending on the current state of the market. For example, if the market is in a downturn the firm could offer bonds and/or closed-end, fixed-income funds to its clients. These investments are sold under something called a *syndicate.* This simply means that the brokerage company agrees to hold a supply of that particular investment to market and sell. The firm's advisors then contact their best clients and tell them they have a bond offering that's going to be sold "without commission." They market the offering as an in-house deal that they have exclusive rights to offer.

And all of what they tell clients is true except...the parts that are lies. The way they offered the deal sounds like it's a sure win because it's so exclusive. It's a sweet opportunity. Or is it? Turns out there is a commission, but it's not shown as a commission; it's simply added to the price of the bond. As a matter of fact, the commission is as high as three percent on BOTH the buy and the sell.

Remember, when an investment is sold on the stock market after the initial public offering the market dictates the price. In these wire house investments, the price has an added markup that, in effect, is a disguised commission to the broker.

Also remember, while the investment sounds like a sure-fire win it may actually be an average opportunity at best. The investors think they're being given an exclusive offer to get into a great company. They think they're special. At the end of the day, however, they may be hearing the offer first but if they decline, the brokers will go to the next tier of clients and the next and the next until all of the securities are sold. The company is simply using a sales tactic to unload the offering more quickly.

The bottom line is that the brokers are being paid to sell the investment no matter how they sell it, period. And to top it off, many brokers typically will come back to the investors several weeks or months later and say that it's time to get out, for better or worse, whether there is an increase in value or not. That sale (of course) further lines the broker's pocket.

And fleecing doesn't stop there. Many brokerage houses have their own family of mutual funds. Usually, they encourage their agents and representatives to sell those funds and receive a higher commission. Often these funds are inferior to others on the market and do not put the investor in the best possible position.

Some investment vehicles that have state-specific rules provide further opportunities for unscrupulous brokers to profit at their clients' expense. For example, so-called *529 College Savings Plans* potentially carry state tax benefits for the investor. This means if I live in Virginia and contribute to a Virginia 529 plan, a percentage of my investment can be taken as a state tax deduction. Many states follow the same guidelines.

The main problem is this: most states have chosen one fund company to offer these funds. So in the state of Virginia, let's say the 529 plan is offered through XYZ Fund Company. So here is Mr. Honest Broker meeting with a client from Virginia; he feels the state's 529 plan is perfect for his client's tax situation. Of course he can only access the plan's funds through XYZ. Okay, no problem. But what if Mr. Broker works for ABC Fund Company and they are the offering sponsor of the New Jersey 529 plan?

Now the broker is in a predicament because his company is pressuring him to use the New Jersey ABC funds even though his client in Virginia won't receive any tax benefit. In theory it should be no issue, because the broker should put his client into the Virginia plan. Sadly this is often not the case. I see prospective clients with 529 plans from all over the country even though they live in Virginia. Not good.

Just three months prior to this writing, I had a client who had several 529 plans for his children and each plan was from a different state. Why? Because the family broker had changed firms and each time the broker moved, he had the client open a new plan with the newest firm, a plan based in a state other than the state in which the client lived.

Recently the rules pertaining to 529 plans have gotten more strict and so now it's much more difficult for a broker to put a client into the wrong state's plan. But this mismatch was commonplace just a few years ago and does still happen today.

Too Good to be True?

You may have heard of the *equity index annuity* which is still being sold today. This annuity is not necessarily a poor product but it's **not** something investors should put all of their money into. This annuity is an investment, backed by insurance companies, that on the outside looks very attractive. The theory is you make money when the market is good but stay flat when the market is poor.

Here's how it works. Suppose you put $100,000 into an index annuity. The sponsoring insurance company uses part of your money to purchase bonds that pay a fixed interest rate. They then use another part of your investment and/or interest from the bonds to buy S&P 500 options. These options give the insurance company the right to buy the S&P 500 at a certain price, usually at or below the market price where the S&P stands at the time of purchase. If the market goes up, the options make money and so does your annuity. If the market goes down, the options only lose the amount of money that the insurance company paid for the options (they expire worthless).

So what does this annuity look like from the investor's perspective? Well, if the market goes up, the investor will make the market return limited to a certain cap on earnings, usually somewhere between eight and twelve percent per year. If the market goes down the investor won't make any money but won't lose money either. So far, this sounds fairly attractive doesn't it? What's not to like about an investment that only goes up with the market but never down?

These annuities are attractive, but the real questions arise relative to how these annuities are commonly sold. First, these securities are considered a *fixed income investment* so the people who sell them don't even need a securities license. (The investment industry is changing this situation and people who represent index annuities will have to be licensed in the near future.)

Second, many of the agents who have sold these products tell their clients that the product makes high returns with no chance of going down. While it's true the investment won't go down, it typically won't go up all that much either. Because of the cap on the returns and because there will be years of zero percent growth, the long-term returns wind up being much lower than expected, at best usually about 4–7% per year.

True, in a market downturn 4–7% sounds really good. The ethical issue is that many reps tell their clients that the product will make 8–12%. That's simply not the case. Finally, many of these products have very long surrender periods of up to 12–20 years, and very high commissions, typically 8–15%.

Don't get me wrong, many advisors use these investments with good intentions and for all the right reasons. Just be aware that despite what some brokers will tell you, these annuities are not without concerns.

You've often heard people say to beware of something that sounds too good to be true. That admonition is especially true when it comes to money.

I met with an older woman a couple of years ago and found an equity index annuity in her existing portfolio. She had purchased this product from a broker who told her he could "guarantee" her return for a very long time. The "time" part was certainly true as the product had a 17-year surrender period. If she tried to take her money out before the period was up, the surrender charge was over 15%.

When I explained how the product worked she was very upset that she had never been given a lot of critical information. In her case the broker probably made a nice 15% commission. So the woman invested $150,000 and her broker made a ridiculous $22,500.

The reason the surrender period was 17 years is that the insurance company paid so much commission to the broker that they had to keep the product on the books for a longer period for the investment to be profitable.

Many annuities pay brokers a high commission and then hold investors captive for a long time with lengthy surrender periods. Some annuity products have merit and some don't.

Please understand that I'm not saying investors shouldn't use annuities or that brokers shouldn't make a commission. I am, however, a big fan of full disclosure. Advisors have an obligation to make certain that clients know what they're getting into. What's the rationale for the investment? What's the likely **net** return? How long will the investor have to keep the product? There needs to be a compelling reason to utilize the investment beyond just the broker's commission.

Holding on Too Long

It's frightening when I see a portfolio that reminds me of Grandma's house. I'm not saying I don't love Grandma, but at some point she may need to update the furnishings a little. Not infrequently I see an investor who has a significant sum of money in a fund that the famous Peter Lynch used to run. I won't mention the specific fund but you would absolutely recognize the name if you heard it. While it was a great fund in its time, it has since soured. But to witness that an advisor recommended it many years ago and hasn't changed the investment is a true tragedy. That fund went from great to mediocre more than a decade ago.

So why didn't the broker change it? Because he simply lost track of his client and the assets in their account. Quite honestly, he was not watching the account like his client thought he was. (This particular fund may come back into favor, but I would not want my clients to endure the mediocre returns in the meantime.)

This negligence is just as bad as recommending a fund that had a five star track record **last year** or one that **used to be** in *Money Magazine's* annual top fund list. While looking at these lists is a good idea, stopping the research there is not. Your advisor needs to do much more due diligence before you invest in anything. Quite honestly, few do. And then you get stuck with a below average portfolio and worse yet, below average returns.

I'd love to be able to say that I've summarized every dirty little secret out there, but I know there are many more skeletons in the closets of many brokers. I simply wanted to give you some of the common things to look out for. As long as there are new products being offered, some brokers will get greedy and look for a way to skirt the system.

It's no different in any profession involving sales. Do you think every car dealer operates the way the parent company would desire? Some dealerships are honest and straightforward and others are, well…

My overall premise is that it's not productive to harp on what you don't want in your broker, but it's important to look for the things you do want in a good relationship. Many brokers do follow the rules, but you may accidentally stumble upon one who doesn't.

Be proactive, be vigilant, and insist on documentation and full disclosure. You'll be a lot happier in the long run.

SUMMARY

Changing, even for the better, is never easy.

Most of us are not happy with something in our lives, whether it's our relationships, our waistline, our finances, whatever. We generally know that the situation is up to us to fix. But we also realize that to "fix" our situation, we'll have to do something very difficult...CHANGE!

We all hate change even when we know we should. Change is one of the most difficult things in life. And while we may dislike it, change is essential for us to truly grow.

Think about when you were a child and couldn't read. You'd have to ask your Mom or Dad, "What does that sign say?" or "Will you read this comic to me?" You went from not knowing what the jumble of letters meant to being able to read an entire book. It took effort, it wasn't always comfortable, but in the end your life improved. Change led to progress.

What about fitness? Almost everyone at some point in their lives wants to be in better shape. We want to look better, feel better, and live longer. So why don't we exercise? Because of all the habits we'd have to change. If we want to lose weight we'll need to change our diet, change our eating habits, change our workout schedule or start one. We're talking about lots of change.

Clearly such change is extremely difficult. Everyone agrees being fit is better, but the change is just too much. You can see this based on the rising obesity rate in the U.S.

The call to change is the real challenge in *Fire Your Broker*. When you fire your broker it will cause a big change in your financial world.

The thought of this change causes fear and discomfort and inertia.

Everything will be new when you fire your broker. There will be a new contact person, a new statement to read, different investments, different phone numbers, and different websites where you can check account balances. These changes will be a little difficult to get used to.

The secret of any positive change is to focus on the outcome. You always need to remember that you began looking for a new advisor because you were unhappy with the old one. Something caused you to say, "I need a change."

Now you have to trust your judgment and know that the differences may take a little getting used to, but if you've truly followed the principles outlined in this book, you will soon have the relationship you've been looking for.

You'll experience the type of relationship that will help you achieve your goals and one that will give you comfort knowing that your accounts are being honestly and carefully monitored. And maybe, just maybe, you'll sleep better at night.

Just have confidence that having a new advisor will be a little difficult initially but eventually will be the best financial decision you will ever make.

Reasons to Fire Your Broker Now

There are situations when I believe you should fire your broker IMMEDIATELY, if not sooner. Here is a list of some of those things to look for.

1. You always have to initiate communication…your advisor never calls you.

2. Your advisor constantly trades your account making great commissions but not good returns for you.

3. Your advisor or the office staff constantly makes mistakes.

4. Your advisor has a meeting with you but doesn't listen to what you say. (You may discover this in subsequent meetings or correspondence when you're asked the same questions again and again.)

5. Your advisor makes changes you did not agree to or actually said NO to.

6. Your advisor is a one-person operation.

7. Your advisor typically calls you with ideas that will fill his pockets and cost you money.

8. Your advisor has a poor record with FINRA/SEC or has a number of formal complaints.

9. Your advisor wants to put all of your money into one product that pays a high commission.

10. Your advisor is more interested in your money rather than who you are and what your goals are.

11. Your advisor pressures you to decide too quickly. If it feels like you are being sold a timeshare, it may be time to bail.

Many of you may be on the fence about changing your advisor or broker. You may feel that sometimes you're happy with them and sometimes you're not. If you are not sure, just ask the following questions of your broker and of yourself. I believe with some careful introspection, you will find the right solution.

Summary of the Right Questions to Ask

1. Does your advisor really know what your investment objectives are? Are you just another client or does your advisor know your most important life and money-related goals?

2. How many clients does your advisor personally serve? In other words, is the advisor more concerned about your money and a new account or about you? What kind of communication do you receive from the advisor's office?

3. Is your broker a stock picker, trying to find next year's stellar performer or does he or she have a comprehensive system for choosing investments and making portfolio decisions? Is there a better way?

4. What are your advisor's criteria for adding new clients? Are you a good fit?

5. Does your advisor have account minimums or will he or she work with anyone who walks through the door?

6. How is your advisor compensated? Is he fee-based, commission-based or both?

7. Is your advisor sufficiently risk and tax conscious?

8. Does your advisor run an independent and proper business? Does he or she operate as a real business? Can you tell if your advisor is serious about the profession?

9. Does your advisor have a clean record?

10. What is your advisor doing behind your back that benefits him at your expense?

11. Will your financial advisor call you at specific time intervals each year to review your accounts or do you have to initiate the calls? Do you receive a written personalized Investment Policy Statement and Financial Policy Statement?

(For more information, go to www.fireyourbroker.com.)

EPILOGUE:
SOME FINAL THOUGHTS...

I approached the writing of this book with some amount of trepidation... okay, fear. I wanted to improve the industry without offending any of my fellow advisors. As I got more and more into the content I realized that would be impossible.

As I dug into my years of experience for real-life examples, I was forcefully reminded that what I do every day, what every advisor does every working day, is impact the lives of people. I became impassioned about my message and determined to tell the truth as I see it. If some people are offended, well maybe they need to be.

The investing public needs to be educated so they can start making a change and take control.

Writing the book reaffirmed for me the real reason why I'm excited to go to work every day. I have the chance to improve people's lives.

At its best, this profession is a partnership, a partnership that places demands on the advisor and the client. The advisor is a dedicated professional but more than that, he is a friend. He's a friend who calls you not just when the market takes a positive jump, but someone who calls when your daughter graduates from college or when you've lost a loved one. He's someone who locks arms with you in the fight for your future and your dreams.

For your part, you have to determine your personal goals. I frequently talk about how too many people approach investing using the 80/20 rule. They spend 80% of the time planning their investments so they can retire and only 20% (or less) planning what they'll actually do when they retire.

At its best, financial planning is an exciting ride into your dreams. Yes there will be twists and turns in the road, there will be uphills and downhills, but you and your advisor should be focused on things that stir your blood.

There is nothing in my profession more thrilling than helping someone get in touch with a future that really has meaning for them. When I can help an investor see a life ahead that makes them not fear the future but be excited about it, and then help them accomplish that future, there is no greater reward. I feel I am fulfilling my life's purpose.

My personal approach to planning starts with a fundamental belief in the power of each individual to control his or her destiny. I firmly believe that people with a clear vision, the right priorities, a belief in themselves, and surrounded by supportive friends, can accomplish most anything.

I'd encourage you, regardless whether or not you fire your broker, to believe in your ability to control your future. Know that you can accomplish whatever is important to you and make it happen.

Life is not about money and jobs, it's about family, friends, and accomplishing your dreams. We all tend to get lost in the day-to-day and we lose perspective on what's really important to us. We forget what we really want to accomplish in life.

I believe in your ability to accomplish a great life. I pray that this book has contributed in some small way to putting you on that path.

Thank you, Kelly

ACKNOWLEDGEMENTS

Writing a book, on the surface, is simply putting thoughts to paper. That sounds easy enough. But the true process from start to finish takes much more work than I ever imagined. But believe me, the writing is not just my effort, it's work that can be accomplished only with support and help from so many others.

That assistance came in the form of freeing my schedule so I could write, providing ideas when my idea well had dried up, helping me think of other more eloquent ways to say things, and encouraging me to keep going when I was tired of thinking and rethinking and rethinking again. For all of the following people I want to give you the ultimate kudos for being such a wonderful part of my life and for your support over the last year.

First, I have to thank my family: my wife Kim, daughter Codie, and my two sons, Carter and Connor. They were the ultimate contributors as they were the ones that gave up "husband" time and "Daddy" time while I was creating. Kim, in the final stretch of this effort, kept me laser-focused and kept all of the "production" people on track. I love my family dearly and am looking forward to once again spending some quality time with them.

I am forever grateful to my mother who always told me that I "can do anything I put my mind to!" Without her telling me that since I was a kid, I would not have become the person I am.

I need to thank a sincere coach and true friend, Elsa Bonstein, who is also a writer, a wonderful person, a great (but messy) cook, and yes, my mother-in-law. She encouraged me to write and also pushed me to "get it done." Gene, my father-in-law, also helped with his thoughts and editorial advice. Both knew how important this creation was to me and helped me accomplish the task.

My editor, Todd Rainsberger, took my words when they made sense to **me** but to no one else, and rearranged them to get my points across. Without him, my story may have been incomprehensible.

My team at Campbell Wealth Management kept the ship afloat while I wrote, and ran the office when I was sometimes a little distant in thought.

My coaching group from PEAK taught me many of the business strategies that allowed me to even write this book.

Other coaches I want to thank are Dan Sullivan, Sarano Kelley, Tony Robbins, Ron Carson, Chet Holmes, Lou Holtz and the many others who will not even remember me. But I certainly remember what I have read, heard, and learned from them.

Andy Andrews sat for five hours in a car and listened to me rant and rave about people's true potential. He provided the impetus and inspiration to get my message out.

My clients are an important group on this list. They give me the reason to do what I do. Their lives have provided stories to write about and goals to help accomplish. Those good people taught me lessons in life that I am not sure I would have ever learned on my own. I am also appreciative of those folks who have never been clients but shared their life stories with me.

I'm grateful to Athena Golianis and her team who helped me put a face on the book. Joe Anthony helped get my message out to the world by putting me in front of many audiences. Jill Stelfox, CEO, marketer, and a great person provided positive inspiration as well as excellent ideas to get my message out.

My CEO group has been instrumental in getting me to take action on this project. I didn't always take their advice (as I'm sure they will agree) but when I did, great things happened. What wonderful entrepreneurs.

Finally, and I think most importantly, I want to thank my step-father, Richard Alley. He was truly a father to me. He took me under his wing and helped me when I needed it most. He also was one of those that lost almost everything because of a scoundrel of a broker. He's the real reason you're reading this book and he has so much to do with the crusade I'm on to rid the world of crooks and incompetents in our business.

A project of this magnitude reminds me how truly blessed I am to be surrounded by so many wonderful people.

Thank you.

ACTION PLAN

for

more

information

visit our website

www.**fire**your**broker**.com

NOTES